URBAN SPRAWL AND GIS

URBAN SPRAWL
AND
GIS

By

Dr. R. Basawaraja
Professor
Department of Civil Engineering
Principal of HKES
SLN College of Engineering
Raichur (Karnataka)
(INDIA)

&

Dr. K.B. Chari
MS, M.Phil & Ph.D.
(GIS & Remote Sensing)
Pondicherry (Central) University
Tamil Nadu
(INDIA)

D P H

DISCOVERY PUBLISHING HOUSE PVT. LTD.
NEW DELHI-110 002

Published by:

Namit Wasan

DISCOVERY PUBLISHING HOUSE PVT. LTD.

4383/4B, Ansari Road, Darya Ganj
New Delhi-110 002 (India)
Phone : +91-11-23279245, 43596064-65
Fax : +91-11-23253475
E-mail : discoverypublishinghouse@gmail.com
namitwasan9@gmail.com
sales@discoverypublishinggroup.com

website: www.discoverypublishinggroup.com

***First Edition:* 2016**

ISBN: 978-93-5056-778-4

Urban Sprawl and GIS

Printed at:
Infinity Imaging Systems
Delhi

DEDICATION

To My Parents

— Dr. R. Basawaraja

To My Wife Anu Pallavi and My Daughter Pranati

— K.B. Chari

PREFACE

The biggest challenge for science and technology in the 21st century is to ensure adequate housing, transportation services, sanitation and health in a habitable urban environment in developing countries. Urban sprawl is seen as one of the potential threats for such development.

This book demonstrates the techniques of Remote Sensing and Geographic Information Systems (GIS) for analysing the spatiotemporal patterns, causes and concerns of urban sprawl of a typical city with special reference to Raichur city of Karnataka, India.

Raichur City is no exception to the frantic and feverish urban sprawl that has characterised the increasing metropolitanization of Indian cities. In the present study, an attempt has been made to study the urban sprawl pattern of Raichur City vis-à-vis the infrastructure and other utility services such as: water supply, sanitation, power transmission, and agriculture using the state-of-the-art remote sensing techniques and Geographical Information Systems.

The authors strongly believe that this book would serve as a compendium of reference to the young scientists and scholars of Sociology, Geography and Geo-informatics.

– Authors

CONTENTS

ABBREVIATIONS

NOMENCLATURE	Expanded Form
APMC	Agricultural produce marketing Committee
AME	Academy of Medical Education
ASTRA	Application of Science and Technology to Rural Areas
CAD	Computer Aided Drafting
CAGR	Compounded Annual Growth Rate
CC	Cement Concrete
CGI	Common Gateway Interface
CMC	City Municipal Council
CRM	Customer Relationship Management
DEM	Digital Elevation Model
DTM	Digital Terrain Model
EMPACT	Environmental Monitoring for Public Access and Community Tracking
EMS	Environmental Management System
ERDAS	ERDAS IMAGINE is a remote sensing application
ERP	Enterprise Resource Planning
ESRI	Environmental Systems Research Institute
FOSS	Free and Open Source Software
GIS	Geographical Information System
GUI	Graphical User Interface
HTTP	Hypertext Transfer Protocol

IB	Inspection Bungalow
IDSMT	Integrated Development for Small and Medium Towns
IISc	Indian Institute of Science
INR	Indian National Rupee
ISO	Indian Standards Organisation
ITI	Industrial Training Institute
KHB	Karnataka Housing Board
KPC	Karnataka Power Corporation
KPCL	Karnataka Power Corporation Limited
KSRTC	Karnataka State Road Transport Corporation
LISS-III	Linear Imaging and Self Scanning
LPA	Local Planning Area
MDR	Major District Roads
MLD	Million Liters Per Day
MNDNR	Minnesota Department of Natural Resources
NASA	National Aero space Administration
NAUTILUS	Northeast Applications of Useable Technology In Land Use Planning for Urban Sprawl
NDC	Number of Different Classes
NGO	Non-Governmental Organisation
NRSC	National Remote Sensing Centre
OGC	Open Geospatial Consortium
OGC-WMS	Open GIS Consortium Web Map service
OPEC	Oil Producing and Exporting Countries
PCU	Passenger Car Units
PGR	Population Growth Rate
PUC	Pre-University Course
QGIS	Quantum GIS : Open source GIS
ReC	Raichur e-City
RTO	Road Transport Office
SH	State Highway
SLN	Sarojini Leeladharan Nair
SOI	Survey of India
SOM	Server Object Manager

TIN	Triangulated Irregular Network
UDPFI	Urban Development Plans Formulation and Implementation Guidelines
UGD	Underground Drainage
ULB	Urban Local Body
UMN	University of Minnesota
UNESCO	United Nations Educational, Scientific and Cultural Organization
URL	Uniform Resource Locator
UT	Union Territory
VAT	Value Attribute Table
VDF	Vehicle Damage Factor
WBM	Water Bound Macadam
MNC	Multi National Company
WTO	World Trade Organisation

1

INTRODUCTION

The world will be more urban in the early part of this century on account of large population movements from rural to urban. Over 70 million people migrate from rural to urban areas every year. At this rate, more than 60 per cent of the world's population will be living in cities by around the year 2030.[1]

People move to urban spaces for many different reasons, assumed advantages such as: educational, employment and business opportunities. Urbanization was initially considered to improve the quality of human life by reaping the benefits of advances in technology. However, problems have quickly emerged such as: traffic congestion, increased pollution, limited real estate, decreasing resources and expensive cost of living (Plate 1.1 to 1.3). Due to these probable side effects of urbanization, people started moving from cities to the fringes of urban areas giving rise to new phenomena called urban sprawl.

WHAT IS URBAN SPRAWL?

Urban sprawl has been broadly defined by Nelson and Duncan[2] as unplanned, uncontrolled, and unco-ordinated single-use development that doesn't provide for an attractive and functional mix of uses and/or is not functionally related to surrounding land uses and which variously appears as low density ribbon or strip, scattered, leapfrog, or isolated development (Figure 1.1).[3,4]

The land-use pattern of a sprawl has low values on one or more of eight distinct dimensions of land-use patterns:

1. Density.
2. Continuity.
3. Concentration.
4. Nuclearity.
5. Diversity.
6. Proximity
7. Centrality.[5]

DYNAMICS OF URBAN SPRAWL

The dynamics of urban sprawl are complex and complicated. Urban sprawls are generally driven by a combination of factors that work progressively and factors that happen irregularly such as: rapid changes in the land-use pattern, land-use policies, and infrastructure.

The Role of Land Value

All else being equal, more sprawls occur where land values are lower.[2, 6, 7, 8] In areas that produce high-value agriculture crops, farmers will bid successfully against low-density house builders and maintain the land in agriculture. The relationship also works the other way around: the only crops on which farmers can profit in the shadow of urbanization are those that fetch fairly high prices.[9] Higher house values, similarly reflect and perpetuate higher land values. When land owners know that builders can sell their products at a high price, they raise their selling price for land accordingly. Builders respond to higher land prices by raising density within limits imposed by consumer demands and zoning restrictions.

Infrastructure Investments

Several studies have drawn connections between infrastructure investments and reductions in urban densities. In the earlier 1900s, most urban dwellers limited their search for housing to the areas they could reach by foot; they were also somewhat confined by the proximity of community wells. However, rapid industrial growth and the sub-sequent advent of mass-transportation has rapidly catalyzed the growth of urbanization.

The infrastructure facilities such as: electricity, water supply and sewerage; and the subsidies offered by the local municipalities also influence the growth of urbanization.

Source: http://agmetalminer.com/2011/01/14/the-growth-of-cities-how-urban-sprawl-in-china-and-india-moves-markets

Source: http://www.inmagine.com/stockconnection-006/ptg00106942-photo

Plate 1.1: Panorama view of a Typical City (above) and Aerial view of Freeway Cutting through Los Angeles Urban Sprawl

Source: http://www.guardian.co.uk/environment/2009/dec/02/india-reveal-carbon-emission-target

Source: Photograph of Raichur city taken from the Hillock behind Raichur Bus Stand

Plate 1.2: Typical view of Traffic Jam of a City (above) and Aerial view of Urban Sprawl in Raichur City

Source: http://devpolicy.org/sustainable-urbanisation-sustainable-urban-health-20130110/urban-sprawl-india

Plate 1.3: Asia's Largest Slum Dharavi, Mumbai (above) and Lykavittos Hill and Athens Urban Sprawl Viewed from the Acropolis

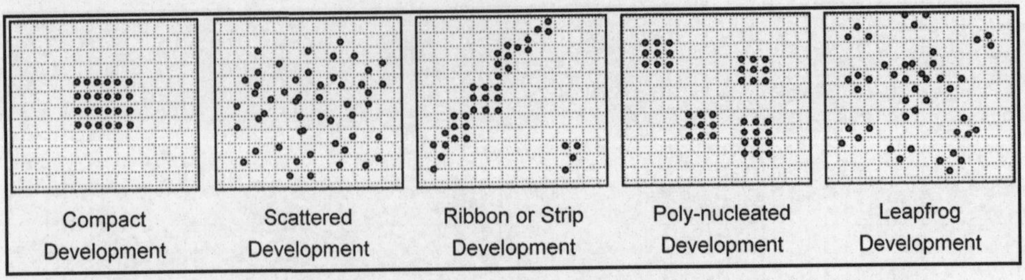

Fig. 1.1: Types of Urban Sprawl-based on the Spatial Pattern

Land-use Fragmentation

Several forms of land-use fragmentation have been suggested as additional contributors to sprawl. Among these, fragmentation of farm ownership leads to a more scattered development pattern than would otherwise occur. Because, farmers decisions about when to sell for development do not necessarily coincide with their neighbors decisions. Whereas, vast land of single ownership can be planned for a relatively high density development, as suggested by Peiser.[10]

Land-use Policies

Often, local governments' land-use policies have been hypothesized and sometimes found, to influence land-use patterns. Fischel[11] cites the work by Moss[12] and Sheppard[13] which shows that suburban development constraints probably induce sprawl.

It matters how local governments pay for the new growth. High levels of public debt and heavy reliance on property taxes both indicate that residents subsidize new development and hence are associated with more sprawls.[14]

Land-use Control

The spatial effects of land-use controls probably depend on the type of control. Zoning for large lots, limiting issuance of building permits, and establishing moratoria on development, for instance, can limit the supply of new housing in the jurisdictions. Demand for housing that goes unsatisfied because of the control will probably be satisfied in another location. However, empirical studies provide mixed evidence on whether development will occur as infill in the existing urbanized areas or as sprawl in newly developed areas.

Often, reduction of sprawl is the goal of other land-use controls. Urban growth boundaries, for example, are supposed to create more compact urban areas.[2] Studies of Oregon's growth boundaries show that they have contributed to increased density in some metropolitan areas.[8]

ISSUES RELATED TO URBAN SPRAWL

Sprawl imposes considerable economic, emotional, aesthetic, and physical costs on the residents of the urban areas that result from the changes in the land-use, environmental pollution, loss of wildlife habitats, increase in ambient temperature and other public health impacts.

Land-use Changes

The rate at which land is converted to non-agricultural uses exceeds the pace of economic development is considered to be an indicator of sprawl. Sprawl has been criticized for eliminating agricultural lands, spoiling water quality, and causing air pollution.[15,16] Symmetrical growth of urban centres consumes agricultural land adjacent to these, resulting in lower agricultural productivity. Besides taxing the groundwater resources available for an urban centre, an increase in the paved area severely reduces the groundwater recharge potential, leading to situations which may prove to be potential catastrophes.[17]

Environmental Pollution

Decentralization is a trend indicative of urban sprawl. The present day industrial, commercial, and residential areas are no longer necessarily a part of the urban core.[18] These types of development are often found in low-density areas that are separated from the major urban area by large tracts of homogeneous land. Hence, the needs for larger transportation networks which in turn create greater dependency on automobiles resulting in air pollution. Laying of new roads leaves the precious farmlands unprotected attracting the commercial and residential developers leading to the strip development of urban sprawl.[19]

Extensive road network and built-up area increases imperviousness of the soil leading to higher run-off causing water pollution and poor ground recharge leading to water scarcity.[20]

Loss of Wildlife Habitats

One of the significant threats to environmental resources is the loss of habitat. Urbanisation alters landscapes and fragments prior patterns of land-use and land-cover, dramatically reducing the amount of habitat, the size of the remaining patches of habitat, and the degree of connectedness among the remaining patches. Land development increases the distances between remaining fragments of habitat, making interactions between isolated populations of plants and animals difficult and hazardous. Sprawl not only consumes wildlife habitats, but also degrades adjacent habitats with light and noise pollution emanating from developed areas.

The Heat Island Effect

On warm days, urban areas can be -14.4° to -22.2°C (6°-8°F) warmer than surrounding areas, an effect known as an urban heat island. The heat island effect is caused by two factors. *First,* the dark surfaces such as: roadways and rooftops efficiently absorb heat from sunlight and reradiate it as thermal infrared radiation; these surfaces can reach temperatures of 10° to 21.1° C (50°-70°F) higher than surrounding air. *Second*, urban areas are relatively devoid of vegetation, especially trees that would provide shade and cool the air through evapo-transpiration. As cities sprawl outward, the heat island effect expands, both in geographic extent and in intensity.

Public Health Impacts

One of the cardinal features of sprawl is driving, reflecting a well-established close relationship between lower density development and more automobile travel. In a less dense sprawl, the average person, drivers and non-drivers, travel more miles in a car or two wheeler each day than in a dense sprawl.[21]

The health hazards of commuting long distances include: mental health toll – stress and stress-related health problems, and even physical ailments. Evidence links commuting to back pain, cardiovascular disease, and self-reported stress. As people spend more time on more crowded roads, an increase in these health outcomes might be expected. One possible indicator of such problems is road rage, defined as events in which an angry or impatient driver tries to kill or injure another driver after a traffic dispute.[22]

Numerous studies are indicating that urban sprawl reduces physical activity and promotes obesity. It is likely that post-world war II, zoning and design guidelines overly separate work and shopping destinations from housing, forcing people to drive rather than walk. Other research shows that streets without sidewalks and large-lot zoning further discourage physical activity. This contributes to the current obesity epidemic in the United States.[23]

Though automobile use offers extraordinary personal mobility and independence, it comes with health hazards, including: air pollution, vehicle crashes and pedestrian injuries and fatalities.

Social Impacts

As per Putnam[24], the simple fact of more driving time means less time with family and friends, and less time to devote to community activities. Putnam estimates that each additional 10 minutes of driving time predicts a 10 per cent decline in civic involvement.

Suburban development patterns often feature considerable economic stratification. Many housing developments are built to specific price ranges, so that buyers of premium prices homes are effectively segregated from those at the bottom of the economic ladder. This pattern creates income homogeneity within neighbourhoods but may intensify income inequality across metropolitan areas.

AND YET SPRAWL HAS ITS BENEFITS!

Sprawling offers access to less-expensive housing and opportunities for house ownership at the periphery of metropolitan areas. It provides congestion management in automobile - dominated metropolitan areas by creating the suburban-to-suburban trip and by better equalizing the percentages of the commuting population involved in reverse and forward commutes.[25]

The infrastructure and land conversion costs associated with sprawl are high and yet the quality of life is better and housing costs are lower in locations characterized by sprawl development.

QUANTIFICATION OF URBANIZED LANDSCAPES

In recent years, understanding the dynamics of sprawl, quantifying them and sub-sequently predicting the same for a future period has attracted significant interest of researchers. The advent of information technologies and geospatial technologies has provided a plethora of qualitative and quantitative spatial analytical tools for measuring urban sprawl.

Although various studies have been dedicated to measure and monitor the growth and sprawl of urban forms, they have limitations in capturing the characteristics of urban sprawl. Several authors have decried the lack of quantitative approaches to defining sprawl, yet few have developed comprehensive ways to measure sprawl. Several characteristics are attributed to sprawl; therefore, their detection and measurement provides a means by which to delimit the spatial extent of sprawl and quantify its magnitude. These traits include:

- Strip and leapfrog development.
- Fragmented habitats and land-use patterns (patchiness).
- Poor accessibility between adjacent land-uses/segregated land-uses.
- Lack of functional open spaces.
- Automobile dependence and weak public transportation systems.
- Rural to urban land conversion rates that exceed population growth rates.
- Higher rates of energy consumption than more compact settlement forms.
- Increased tax burdens and costs in delivering public services over time.[27, 28]

Some researchers have employed an array of indicators, including land-use conversion, population change, traffic and vehicles, miles traveled, energy consumption, and fiscal measures.[29] Other researchers focused on measuring sprawl through the use of population data and detailed land-use data.[30] The physical expressions and patterns of sprawl on landscapes can be detected, mapped, and analyzed using remote sensing and geographical information system.[31, 32, 33]

Visualizing Urban Sprawl

As there is a lack of universal definition of urban sprawl, a map of urban or built land is an adequate starting point in studying urbanization. A map provides the visual aspect from which studies on urban sprawl can begin in relation to urban growth. Mapping that involves a temporal signature in which two or more time periods are used for comparing amounts of urbanization can reveal the extent of urbanization over a given period of time.[34]

A case study in Gombak District, located in the Klang Valley which is a rapidly growing region in Malaysia, has been described by Ahmed N. M. L. *et al.*, [26] where land-use planning scenarios were generated based on specified planning policies. The planning scenarios were then evaluated by using a Decision Support Software - Definite, to improve the quality of decision-making through the selection of better alternatives. GIS provided a strong platform for decision-makers in its role as the main component in Planning Support System (PSS) and Decision Support System (DSS).

Built-up Area as An Indicator of Urban Sprawl

Typically, conditions in environmental systems with gross measures of urbanization are correlated with population density with built-up area.[35, 36] The percentage of an area covered by impervious surfaces such as: asphalt and concrete is a straightforward measure of development and these surfaces can be easily detected and interpreted in remotely sensed data in developed countries.[37] In certain localities of developing countries, sprawl is also characterized by slums (region with poor housing and amenities), which can also be quantified using remotely sensed data.

The population in the region also influences sprawl. The proportion of the total population in a region to the total built-up of the region is a measure of quantifying sprawl. Epstein *et al.*,[38] also employed a similar technique for mapping suburban sprawl and compared the result with rural and urban centres. Thus, sprawl is characterized by an increase in the built-up area along the urban and rural fringe and this attribute gives considerable information for understanding the behaviour of such phenomenon. Earlier studies carried out in different parts of the world highlight and conform that the built-up area could be used as fairly accurate parameter for urban sprawl analyses. The other parameter that is considered as an indicator of urban sprawl is the night-time data captured with the help of radars or geo-stationary satellites. [39, 40]

In the case of Madurai city of India, an interesting aspect has governed the spread of sprawl.[41] The growth of the city is based on Meenakshi Amman temple as a pivot. Earlier, the development was uniform around the temple and the road network established was regular in shape. So the residential and commercial activities were spread evenly in all directions. As a result the pattern of urban expansion was radial. Later, due to rapid population growth and restriction imposed on the buildings, since no construction should be higher than the towers of Meenakshi Amman temple, eventually it lead to enormous horizontal expansion towards south of city due to the presence of River Vaigai at North. The connectivity between south and north was poor. To develop the northern part of the city, various measures have been taken such as: establishing and shifting many public and semi public organizations such as: Collector Office, Corporation Office, District Court, High Court and Government Hospital to the north. The road network was improved by constructing bridges over river Vaigai and interlinking the highways and major roads. The transport system was improved by locating two main bus terminals - Mattuthavani and Anna Bus stand. The improvement in road network has caused the pattern of sprawl to linear development.

Landscape Metrics

The physical expressions and patterns of sprawl can be detected, mapped, and analyzed using remote sensing data and GIS.[37] The patterns of sprawl can be described using a variety of metrics and through visual interpretation techniques. Characterization of urbanized landscapes over time and computation of spatial indices that measure dimensions such as: contagion, the patchiness of landscapes, fractal dimension, and patch shape complexity are done statistically by NAUTILUS (Northeast Applications of Useable Technology In Land-use Planning for Urban Sprawl) [31, 32, 42] and Fragstats.[43]

Galster *et al.*,[5] employed metrics to describe land development along six geographical dimensions:

1. Density.
2. Continuity.
3. Concentration.
4. Centrality.
5. Nuclearity.
6. Diversity.

Density

Density is the amount of low-density development as a ratio or percentage of total developed land. Higher ratios of low-density development to total developed land indicate sprawl, whereas lower ratios indicate more compact, 'smarter' growth patterns.

Continuity

Continuity reflects the degree to which urban development is spatially contiguous or discontinuous, the latter being reflective of leapfrog sprawl.

Concentration

Concentration is the extent to which development is concentrated on a relatively small portion of a jurisdiction's total land area; low levels of urban concentration provide evidence of sprawl.

Centrality

Centrality indicates the degree to which development is sited close to a jurisdiction's most intensely developed areas or designated growth areas.

Nuclearity

Nuclearity concerns the organization of urban growth around one or several concentrated employment centres: the greater the numbers of employment centres, the more decentralized and sprawling the development patterns.

Diversity

Diversity reflects the mixture of housing and employment opportunities in a given area. One characteristic of sprawl is the segregation of land-uses. In this case, diversity indicates the degree to which residential land-uses are removed from employment – generating land-uses such as: offices, retail stores, businesses, and industrial land-uses. The more separate these land-uses, the longer the commuting distances between homes and employment opportunities. Low diversity denotes sprawl; high diversity denotes more compact patterns of development.[5]

Shannon's Entropy (Hn)

In spatial parlance, entropy (E) is linked to the dispersion of the spatial variable in a given region or boundary and can be measured by Shannon's entropy (Hn). This index reflects the concentration or dispersion of spatial variable in a specified area, to measure and differentiate types of Sprawl. The Shannon's entropy model is developed within the integration of remote sensing and GIS. The advantages of the entropy method are its simplicity and easy integration with GIS.

Shannon's entropy (Hn) can be used to measure the degree of spatial concentration and dispersion exhibited by geographical variable.[44] Cities and towns with higher entropy values are characterized as more sprawled because they exhibited more dispersed development. A series of entropy measures through time can be used to determine changes in the degree to which a city's development is dispersed or compact. Entropy value varies from 0 to 1. If the distribution is maximally concentrated in one region, the lowest value 0 will be obtained. Conversely an evenly dispersed distribution across space will give a maximum value of 1. The dispersal of built up areas from a city centre will lead to an increase in entropy value. This gives a clear picture of whether land development is toward a more dispersed or compact pattern.

The Shannon's entropy (Hn) is given by the following equation:

$$H_n = -\sum P_i \log_e(P_i) \quad \text{......................(1)}$$

Where P_i is the proportion of the spatial variable in the ith zone and n is the total number of zones.

Since entropy (E) can be used to measure the distribution of a geographical phenomena, the difference in entropy between two different periods of time can also be used to indicate the change in the degree of dispersal of land development or urban sprawl.[45]

$$\Delta E = E_{(t+1)} - E_{(t)} \quad \text{.................................. (2)}$$

The entropy approach was successfully applied in the study of sprawl in the urban areas such as: China[33] and it also has gained much popularity among Indian researchers too. Monitoring the sprawl of Hyderabad city[45] and sprawl analysis along Bangalore-Mysore Highway, National Highway between Udupi and Mangalore by Sudhira *et al.*,[46] are few of the examples.

Urban Sprawl Modeling

Batty *et al.*,[47] have successfully analyzed sprawls using differential equations and developing a model to simulate sprawl using cellular automata for the Ann Arbor, Michigan region. Various issues concerned with quantifying urban sprawl phenomenon are addressed[37, 48] to arrive at a common platform for defining the process. Most of these studies quantify sprawl considering the impervious or the built-up areas as the key indicator of sprawl.

MEASURES TO CONTROL SPRAWL

There appear to be more costs than benefits, even though the magnitude of these costs to the general public is not nearly what has been chronicled in the popular press. On the other hand, the level of resource consumption resulting from development increases and this increase is not related to need.

Though, sprawl is not the villain that it has been portrayed to be, it is without question an unnecessary and increasing drain on natural resources. More-compact development patterns produce savings that are both profound and measurable. It makes sense to pursue these development savings.

Some of the means to move towards planning the goal of more compact cities include:

1. Insofar as sprawl is subsidized, the best way to stop it, may be to make growth 'pay its own way'. Local governments need to develop ever more elaborate systems to replace property tax revenue with charges to developers for the schools, libraries, police, fire stations, parks, roads, storm-water infrastructure and other urban systems that require construction to maintain a given service level as population increases. These 'adequate public facilities' measures should promote higher densities and discourage sprawl as landowners and consumers both seek economies in land.
2. Local governments should identify areas where higher densities are appropriate; create incentives for high-density development to occur there, and work in voluntary councils of government to coordinate land-use policies with neighboring jurisdictions.[14] They can encourage redevelopment of underused and abandoned properties, identify locally owned tax-delinquent properties for rehabilitation and occupancy, and provide additional opportunities for mixed uses in urban and suburban neighborhoods.
3. It is essential to incorporate health considerations into policy-making. Because the health effects of sprawl are unevenly distributed across the population, it is equally essential to incorporate considerations of social justice and equity.

These measures, even if taken-up on piece-meal basis would promote more compact urban areas. If adopted as a broader programme that includes a reduction in subsidies to new growth, they will undoubtedly reduce sprawl in coming generations.

SCENARIO OF URBAN SPRAWL IN INDIA

The process of urbanization in India has been slow but steady. As per 2001 census, only less than one-third of India was urban. Predominantly its urban growth has been due to the enlargement of existing towns at every level and not significantly due to the addition of new towns.

One distinctive feature of India's urbanisation is increasing metropolitanization. India's big cities now account for a large share of total urban population. In 2001, the share of metropolitan cities was 37.8 per cent up from 32.5 per cent in 1991 and 26.4 per cent in 1981. The trend indicates continued urbanisation and metropolitanization in the years to come. It clearly implies that with rapid growth of million plus cities, the problem of land management will be more and more complex as the years pass by.

The processes of technological development, globalisation and population growth accelerate the dynamics of urbanisation process in the developing countries. This accelerated phase of urban transition from rural to urban population in developing countries, population from migration and endogenous growth of those large primate cities and industrial location on their fringes are actually expanding the urban areas. This is mainly due to the rapid growth in the IT sector. Although, IT industry in India has more than three decades of history, its take-off into major software industries is a recent phenomenon. Not all cities in India were able to respond quickly to the demands of these new service industries. This is evident from the fact that the larger metropolitan cities of India - Mumbai, Delhi, and Kolkata have not been as successful as the second rung of cities such as: Hyderabad, Bangalore, Pune and Chennai.

Urban morphology of Indian cities has mostly evolved through the process of intensification in the ancient urban core as well as by the current sprawling into urban corridors and spill over into the rural fringe.

In India, natural growth rates and rural to urban migration are expected to raise the country's urban population from 28 per cent of the total in 2001 to as high as about 45 per cent in 2021 spread over about 4,000 urban agglomerates and towns. In India, only 25.8 million people were urban in 1901, this figure shot up to over 230 million, as per the 2001 census. Many cities in India are characterized by uncontrolled growth. Most of this growth is expected to take place in the nine-mega cities of Mumbai (12 million), Kolkata (4.6 million) and Delhi (9.8 million); Hyderabad, Bangalore, Ahmedabad, Pune and Kanpur together containing 21 million populations.

Even though planned urban growth began quite early in Independent India, it appears to have failed the test of time, more so in the fields of proper management of urban resources. The growth is disproportionate to the infrastructural facilities which, by and large, the civic authorities are unable to meet with. Due to unplanned and unstructured land-use planning, lack of adequate civic services, rapid and random expansion of urban centres along their peripheries leads to serious land-use problems. These have assumed significant importance and need proper planning and management. In this context, prior knowledge of patterns of human settlement and their trends would help the developmental agencies in planning for basic amenities.

THE PRESENT BOOK

Raichur City of Raichur district, Karnataka State, India, is no exception to the frantic and feverish urban sprawl that has characterized the increasing metropolitanization of Indian cities. In the present study, an attempt has been made to study the urban sprawl pattern of Raichur City vis-à-vis the infrastructure and other utility services such as: water supply, sanitation, power transmission, and agriculture using the state-of-the-art remote sensing techniques and Geographical Information Systems.

The objectives of the present study are:

1. To understand the various characteristics of Raichur City – the history, climatic settings, geography, demography, socio-economic indicators, and infrastructure.
2. To delineate the multi-temporal and spatial land-use, land-cover characteristics of Raichur City and its surroundings.
3. To identify the multi-temporal dynamics of sprawl and quantify them such that the impact of sprawl can be assessed on the various characteristics of the city.
4. To predict the probable future of the city in terms of demography and land-use, land-cover.
5. To assess the future demands of the city in terms of infrastructure such as: education, health, play-grounds, parks, recreation facilities, religious facilities, agriculture scenario, industrial scenario, water supply, sanitation, administrative structures, traffic and transportation.
6. To generate GIS database for Raichur city that can aid in the ongoing process of monitoring the sprawl.
7. To develop a stand-alone, web capable multi-utility GIS for Raichur City that would enable easy access to the stake holders and administrators alike.

2

RAICHUR CITY
AN OVERVIEW

INTRODUCTION

Raichur City is the largest urban centre and the district head quarter of Raichur District. The city, categorised as City Municipal Council (CMC), is located 486 km., from Bangalore, the state capital of Karnataka, India (Figure 2.1).

Many districts in India are named after the head quarter town. Similarly, Raichur District's name was derived from its original headquarter town – Raichur. Today, many villagers within and surrounding the district are calling the area by its earlier name, which is Rayachooru. Rayachooru is the destination conquered by Vishnuvardhana during his youth.

Origin of the Word – 'Raichur'

The name of Raichur district has considerable antiquity that can be traced back to the 12th century. The earliest three Hoysala inscriptions, dating back to 1160 AD, indicate that Rayachooru was one of the various forts that Vishnuvardhana conquered. The 3rd of the earliest three Hoysala inscriptions that narrate more of the Rayachooru is found at the Hirehalli located in Belur taluk, Hassan District. It was dated back from 1183 A.D., which is the reigning time of the king of Hoysals, Vira Ballala II.

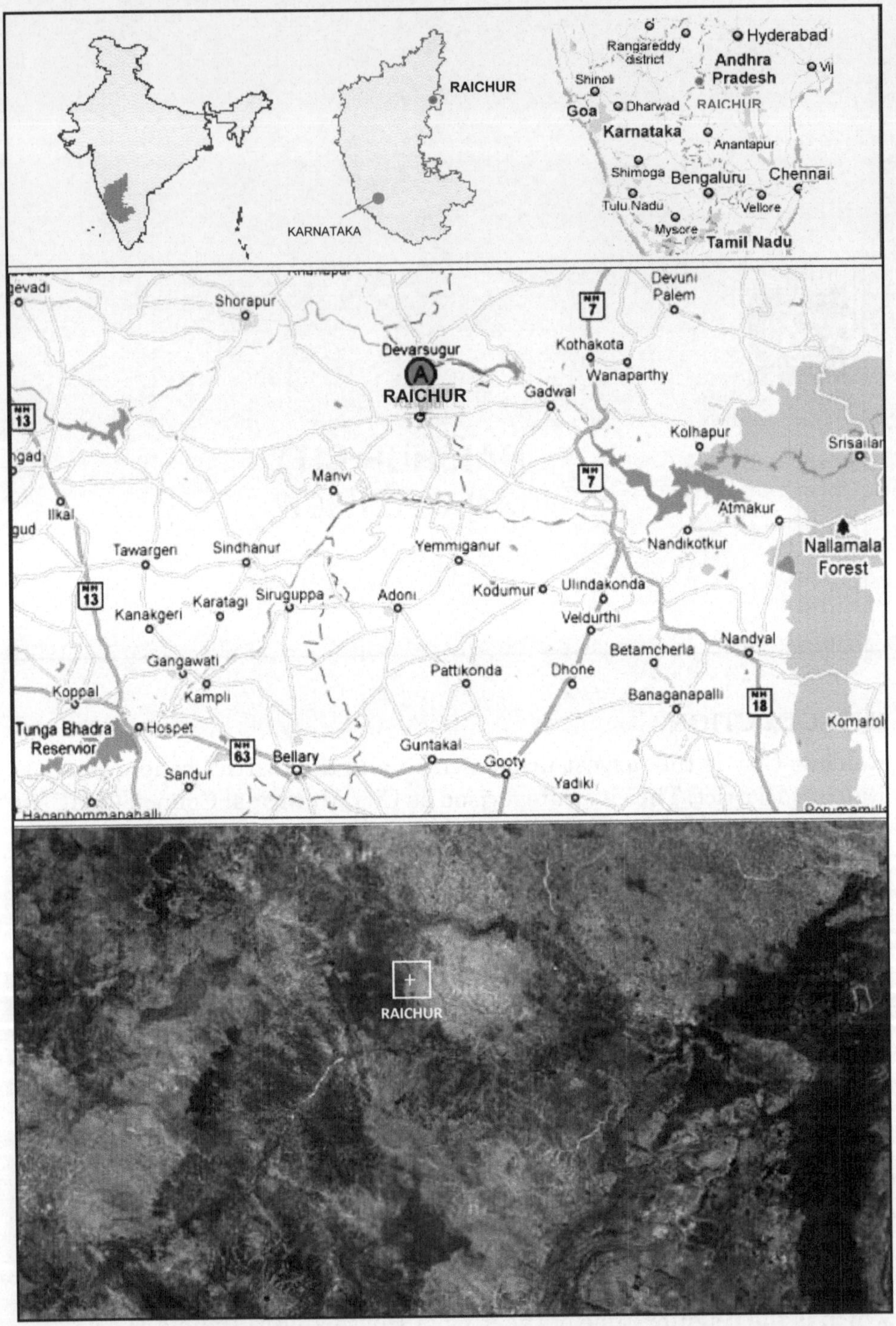

Fig. 2.1: Location Map and Satellite Image of Raichur City[49]

The historical evidences, as deciphered from the inscriptions, point to the fact that the present day Raichur District is the yester years Rayachooru. The term 'racha' was derived from 'raja', which means king. The Rachanoor, Rayachooru, or Rachavoor refers to the place of the King.

In 1294 A.D., the names: Rachanoor, Rayachooru, or Rachavoor have been contracted into Rachooru or Rachoor. It was evident on the Kakatiya inscriptions discovered on the fort wall of the present day Raichur District. The same name continued till 1541 A.D., the period of Vijayanagara 1541 A.D., as evident from the two Kannada inscriptions found in Alampur. During this period, the Rachooru or Rachoor was captured by the king Krishnadevaraya.

Over the centuries, the historical name of Raichur had undergone slight changes in the modern times. The 'ya' had been added between the 'ra' and the 'cha' to make it the present name of the district, which is Rayachooru. The 'ya' became the second syllable of the word 'raya', which refers to a king. In Urdu and Hindi, the reciprocal of the 'raya' is 'rai'.

Another school of thought on the evolution of present day name Raichur, the word 'rai' refers to 'stone' in Telugu. It was given the suffix of 'ooru', which means city or town. As a result, it gave birth to Raiooru name, which refers to city of stones. The Raichur District was said to have many rocks in the vicinity, so the name was given accordingly.[50]

There is another interesting story behind the present day Raichur. The name of Raichur District, they say was derived from 'Naichur', a repeated kind of story that is usually associated with many such forts of India. A hare that was being chased by a dog ('nai') has retorted and killed the dog by tearing it into many pieces ('chur').

HISTORY OF RAICHUR

Historically speaking, Raichur District has three main stages. *First* stage is the prehistoric of Stone Age. *Second* stage is the prehistoric with special richness as depicted in the Mahabharata and Ramayana. *Third* and last stage that overlaps proto-historic period prior to the advent of Buddha.

The history of Raichur dates back to 1294 as it contains a palace-citadel that is believed to be constructed during the same period and a fort (c. 1300) built on a hill 88 m above the surrounding plain (Plate 2.1). In 1489 Raichur became the first capital of the independent kingdom of Bijapur. The area around the town had been a frequent battleground in the early Indian History. Over the centuries, Raichur became a part of various empires. The Mauryas, Chalukyas, Vijayanagara, Bahmanis and the Mughal ruled over Raichur, endowing it with a rich and varied cultural legacy.

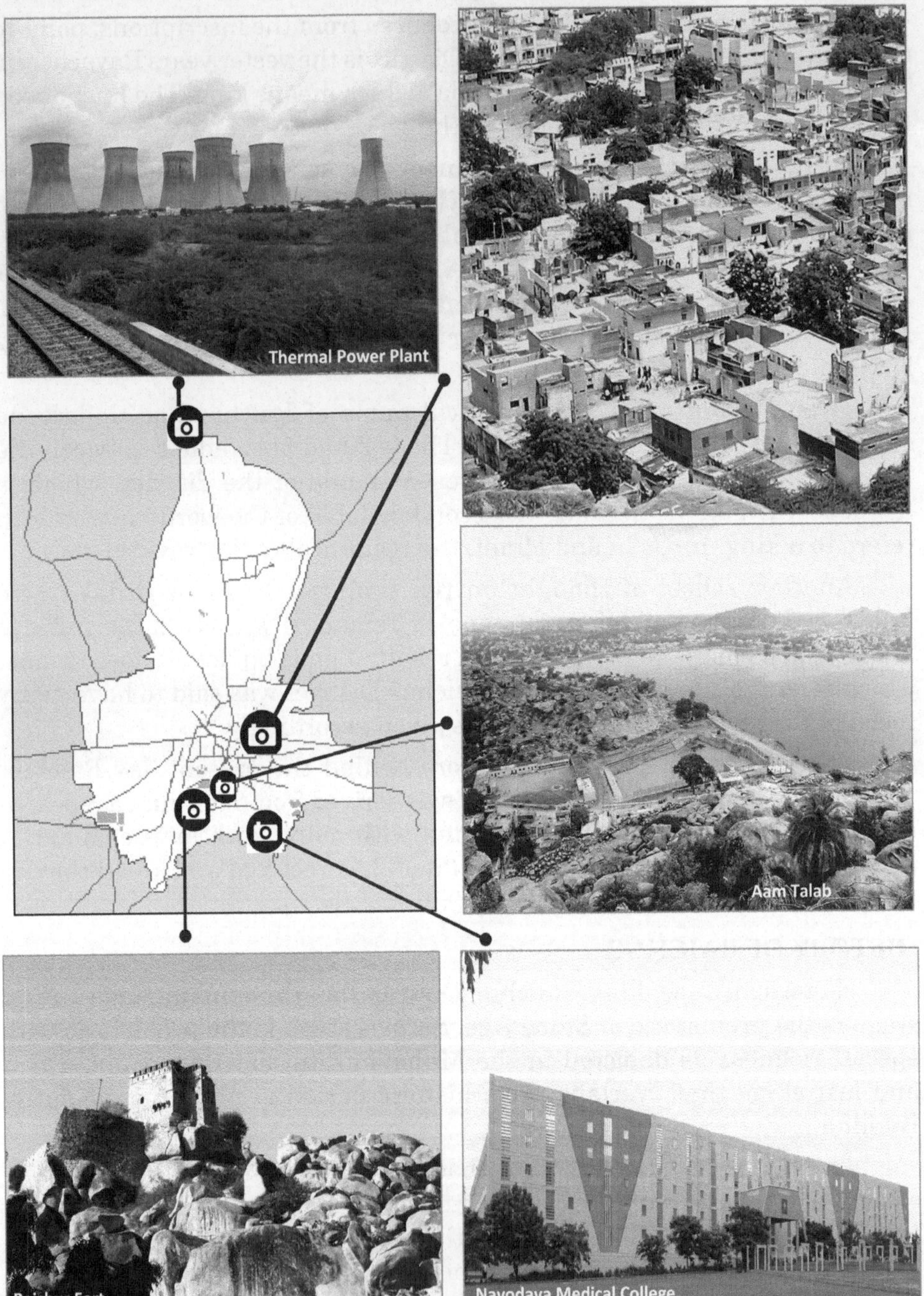

Plate 2.1: A Glimpse of Raichur City

Epigraphically Raichur District is rich, yielding hundreds of inscriptions ranging from the period of Maurya till the end of Muslim period. These inscriptions come in various languages that include Kannada, Prakrit, Sanskrit, Persian, and Arabic. Most of these inscriptions belonged to the dynasties that ruled over Deccan. The most important places from this point of view are the Raichur, Mudgal, Kuknur, Koppal, and Maski.[50]

LOCATION AND GEOGRAPHIC SETTINGS

A city's climate, topography and access to ground water influence the spread of urban sprawl. Hence a detailed description of the climatic and geographic settings has been presented.

General Boundaries

Raichur city is located between 77° 19' 5.17"E to 77° 23' 29.11"E and 16° 10' 28.82"N to 16° 14' 57.07"N, 382 m above MSL, between two major rivers, namely: *(i)* Krishna and *(ii)* Tungabhadra. The city is located on Hyderabad-Anantapur State Highway No. 13.

The district is bounded on the north by the district of Yadgir, on the west by the districts of Bijapur and Bagalkot, on the east by the district of Mahboobnagar (Andhra Pradesh), and on the south by the districts of Kurnool (Andhra Pradesh) and Bellary (Karnataka). The local planning area of Raichur is 215.82 km^2 and the municipal area is 57 km^2.

Climate Settings

The only meteorological observatory in the district is at Raichur. The data of this observatory has been taken as representative of the conditions of the city.

The climate of the district is characterised by dryness for the major part of the year and a very hot summer.[51] The low and highly variable rainfall renders the district liable to drought. The year may be divided broadly into four seasons. The summer season begins from the mid February and extends till the end of May. The rainy season induced by South-west monsoon spreads across the month of June till the end of September.

October and November are the post-monsoon or retreating monsoon months and the period from December till the middle of February is the winter season.

Temperature

December is the coldest month with the mean daily maximum temperature at 29.3° C (84.8°F) and the mean daily minimum at 17.7° C (63.9°F). Nights are generally cool in the season, but day temperatures sometimes reach 35 to 38° C. (Figure 2.2)

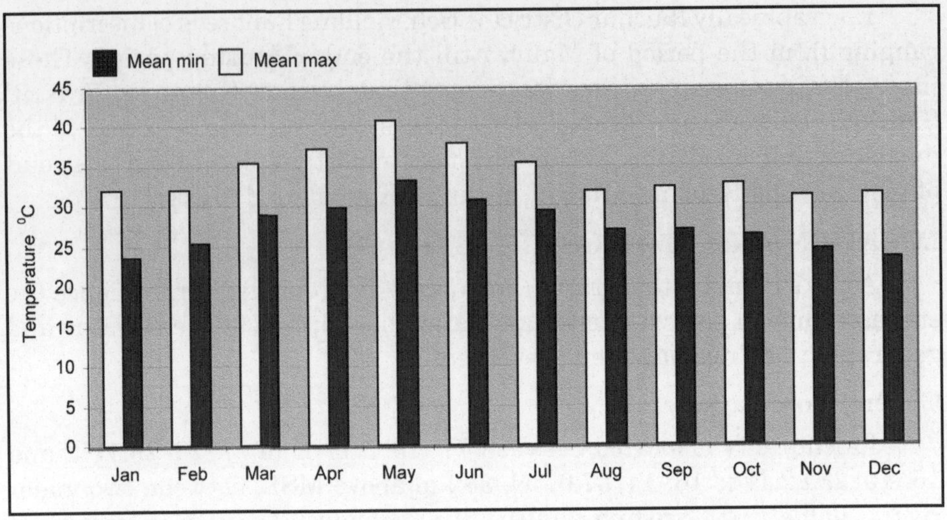

Fig. 2.2: Temperature Pattern during the year 2008 for Raichur city[51]

During the months of summer, mid February to May the day temperature increases rapidly. May is the hottest month, the mean daily maximum temperature being 39.8° C (103.7° F). The heat is oppressive till the onset of the south-west monsoon which usually arrives during the first week of June. Thereafter, the weather becomes moderately cool and continues to be so till the end of the South-west monsoon season. Day temperatures increase in the month of October. From November, both day and night temperatures gradually decrease till December (Figure 2.2).

The highest maximum temperature ever recorded at Raichur was 45.6° C (114.1° F) on 23rd May 1928 and the lowest minimum was 10.0° C (50.0°F) on 14th January 1899 and 13th December 1945.

Rainfall

The normal rainfall (1941-90) is 729 mm with 44 rainy days (District Statistical Office, Raichur). During the south-west monsoon months, *viz*; June to September, the district receives about 71 per cent of the annual rainfall, September being the month with the highest rainfall (Figure 2.3). In the post-monsoon months of October and November also, the district receives some rain. The variations in the annual rainfall from year to year are large as is the case of neighboring districts.

Humidity

The climate of Raichur is dry with low humidity; the months of April and May are the driest (Figure 2.4). The months of August, September and October have higher humidity compared to other months of the year.

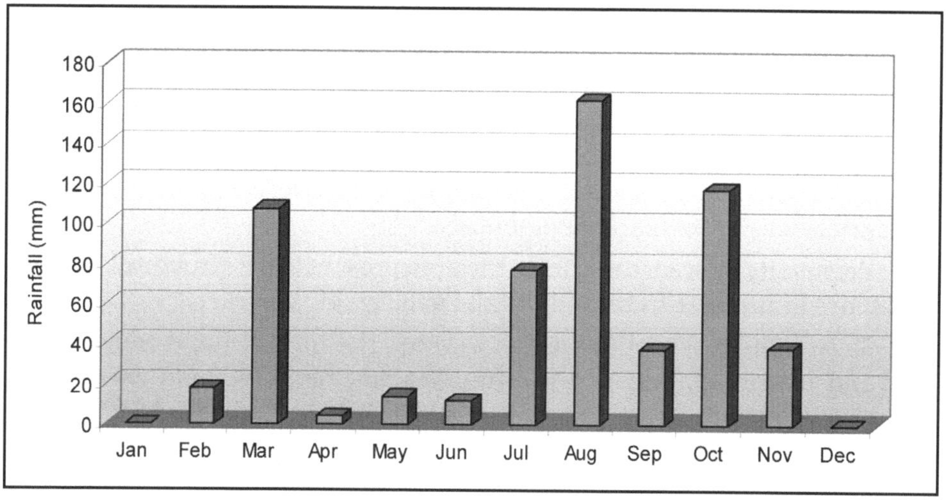

Fig. 2.3: Rainfall Pattern during the Year 2008 for Raichur[51]

Cloudiness

Skies are moderately to heavily clouded during the months of June till September during the south-west monsoon. Clear or partially clouded skies are common during rest of the year.

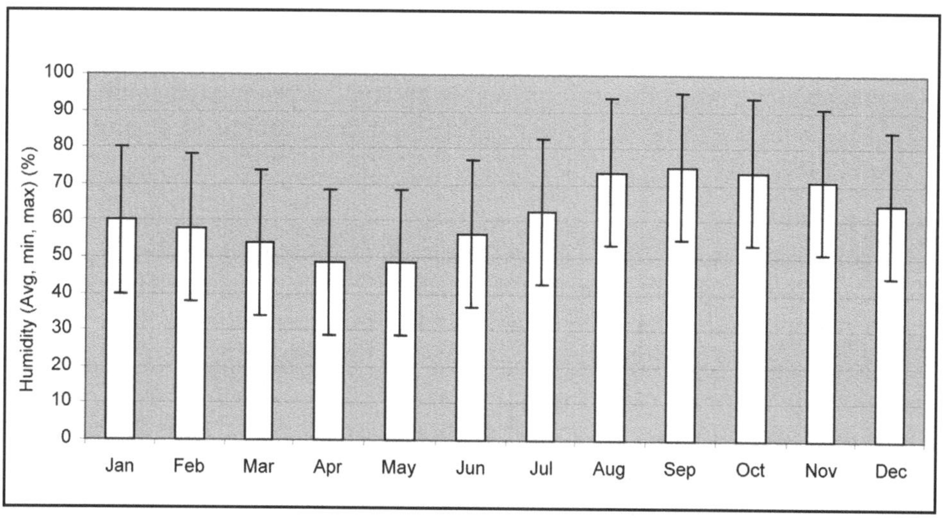

Fig. 2.4: Humidity Pattern during the Year 2008 for Raichur[51]

GEOGRAPHY

Topography

The undulating black cotton soil strips, cut by numerous nalas, characterize the region of the Dharwar schists – which technically are medium or coarse grained metamorphic rocks. These areas, now practically denuded of trees, present a monotonous landscape. While the gneissic region is generally more or less broken and covered with a thin mantle of red loamy soil. Gneissic hills, the sedimentary formations, cover a small belt of the region adjoining the confluence of the Krishna and the Tungabhadra rivers. The rest of the region is represented by flat Deccan plateau, favoring the agriculture growth and settlements.

Regionally viewed, the hills in the area present some structural features which are of interest in relation to the geology of the area:

1. Taking the most south westerly group, the hills of Karigudda, Manvi and Rabhinakal show a continuity along roughly north-west south-east directions.
2. From Sirwar and Yermasagar, running in a roughly south-east direction, may be recognized the hill of Madhugiri, Neermanvi, Gorkal, Kurdi and the one two miles west of Kamalahatti.
3. Between Masarakal and Gabbur, a number of gneissic hills are seen at Kakargal. Jinnapur, Hungundabad. Ramdurga, Jagatkal, Khardigud, Maladkal and Gabbur. The hills around Uttanur are seen to be in line with the south-western group of hillocks in the above areas also the hill-clusters around Kalmala and Kallur, are seen to be situated in the same north-west and South-east disposition as that of the group of gneissic hills enumerated above.
4. The hills around Raichur, which constitute a prominent landmark in the area, may also be seen roughly to display north-west and south-east trends.

Hydrogeomorphology

Under the aegis of *Rajiv Gandhi National Drinking Water Mission,* NRSA (National Remote Sensing Agency, Hyderabad) has surveyed and mapped the hydro geomorphology for Raichur and its surroundings (Figure 2.5).

Raichur is predominantly covered by *Pediplain shallow weathered* geomorphic regions (36%) and *Stripped plains shallow under canal command* area (26%). The remaining region (38%) has *Pediments, Denudational hills, Residual hills* and *Inselberg* formations.

Pediplains Shallow Weathered

These geomorphic units are a result of continuous process of *Pediplanation*. The ground water potential is moderate. The suggested depth for bore wells is 60-80 m for bore-wells during summer or pre-monsoon. The intersection of fracture zones is highly suitable for ground water development. Because of low drainage density, these regions have been recommended as high priority zones suitable for ground water recharge.

The soils are fairly thick, dark greyish brown to black colour, calcareous in composition.

Stripped Plain Shallow under Canal Command

In this region, the ground water is available moderately, the aquifer is made of weathered rock and fissured rock, suitable for dug wells and bore wells. The suggested depth range is 8-12 m (dug wells) and 50-80 m (bore wells). Intersection of fractured zones is highly suitable for ground water development.

Pediment

A gently sloping smooth surface of erosional bedrock with thin veneer of detritus is called pediment. Recharge potential is high and check dams have been suggested as recharge structures. This region is suitable for borewells with depth ranging between 80-100 m. The water quality is potable. Ground water prospects are limited to fracture zones or weathered pockets.

Pediplain Moderately Weathered

In this zone, the recharge conditions are good. The water is potable and suitable for dug wells (8-12 m) and bore wells (50-70 m). Dug wells are preferred in the tank area, because of shallow aquifers and good recharge.

Pediplain Shallow under Canal Command

The recharge potential is good, and the water quality is potable in the case of dug wells and brackish in the case of bore wells. The suggested depth for dug wells is 8-12 m and 50-80 m for bore wells. Dug wells are preferred in the irrigated areas because of shallow aquifers and good recharge from canals.

Pediment Inselberg Complex

The ground water prospects are limited to fracture zones or weathered pockets of pediment area. The water is potable. Bore wells are suggested with a depth of 80-100 m. Check dams are suggested as recharge structures.

Iselberg, Residual hills and *Denudational hills* act as run-off zones and ground water development is not possible in these areas.

Drainage

The Krishna and Tungabhadra rivers make the natural boundaries of Racihur district in the north and south respectively. These rivers make the soils fertile. The drainage pattern is dendrite type developed by the geological formation of granites, gneiss and schist belts of Raichur.

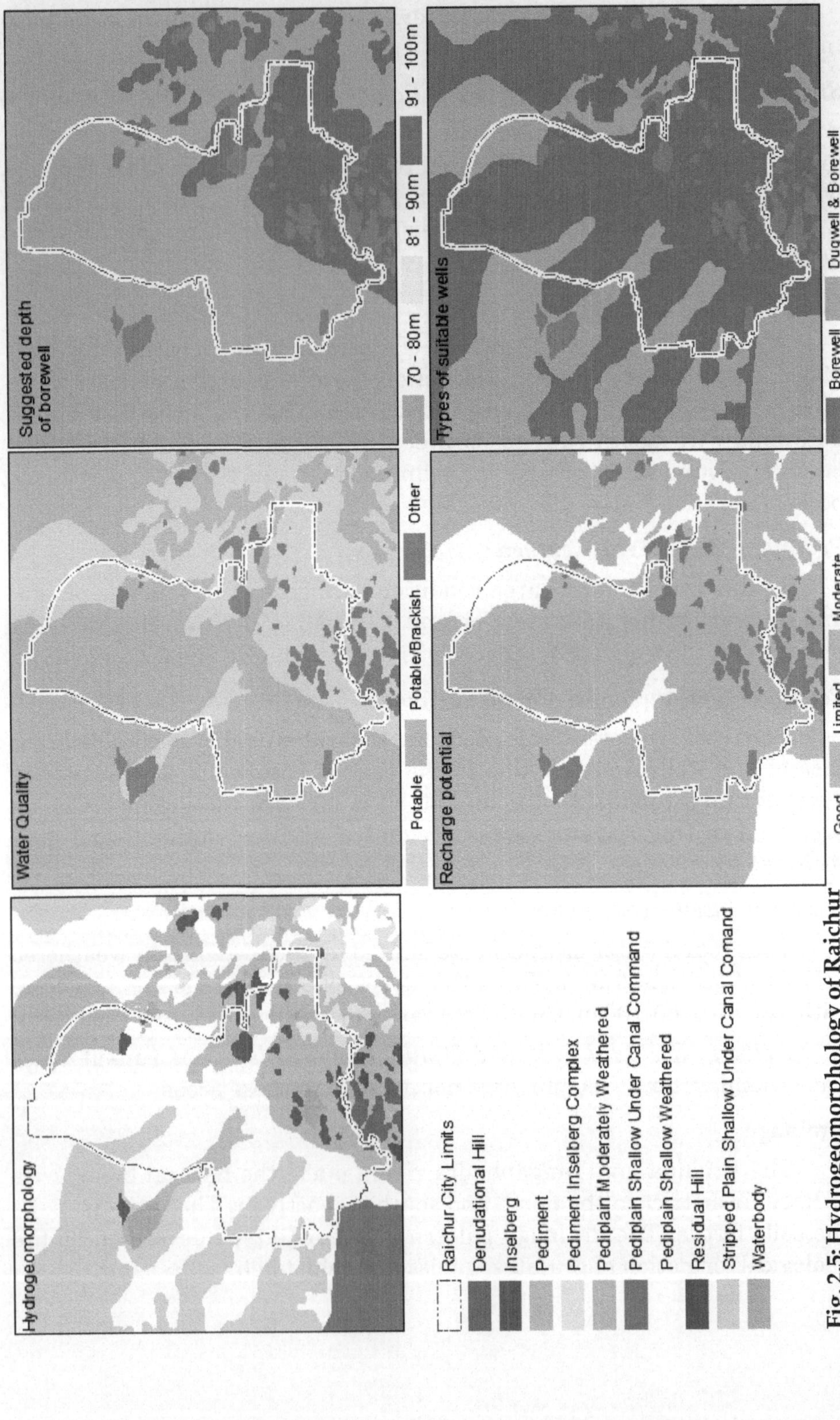

Fig. 2.5: Hydrogeomorphology of Raichur

Soils

The predominant portion of Raichur is covered by clayey soil in the region of *Pediplain Shallow Weathered*. These soils are rich in minerals and organic matters. Poor drainage of these soils has resulted in the formation of saline soils due to the concentration of soda, potash and magnesium.[52]

Seismic Hazard

According to the Bureau of Indian Standard [IS-1893 (Part-1)-2002] and base map as per Digitised Data of Survey of India, Raichur region comes under Seismic Zone II, which is considered low risk.

DEMOGRAPHY

As per the 2001 Census, Raichur city has a population size of 2,07,421. The average population density of the city is 4056 persons per sq km. Total number of households in the town are 37,918.[53] At the Compounded Annual Growth Rate of 2.81 per cent, the CMC's population is projected to swell twice by 2031.

The current sex ratio (female population per 1000 male population) is 960. In 2001 the literacy rate (% of literate population above six years of age) was 49.54 per cent. The male and female literacy rates were 62.2 per cent and 36.84 per cent, respectively.

INFRASTRUCTURE

As Raichur is well connected by rail and road to the important cities like: Bangalore, Mumbai, Chennai, Hyderabad, Ahmedabad and New Delhi. Farmers and traders from the nearby taluks bring their produce to Raichur for local export and sale.

Educational Institutions

Raichur has 11 pre-primary schools, 17 higher primary schools, 7 high schools, 6 PUC colleges, three degree colleges, 2 ITI colleges, 3 polytechnic colleges, 3 Engineering Colleges, 2 Pharmacy Colleges, 2 Dental Colleges and 2 Medical Colleges. Apart from these, the city also has University of Agricultural Sciences, Raichur with various degree, diploma and agricultural courses.

SLN College of Engineering, Navodaya Medical College and AME'S Dental College are a few prominent higher educational institutions.[54]

Industrial Infrastructure

Raichur is known for the production of rice which is of superior quality. There are numerous rice mills which exports high quality rice to different countries.[55] Apart from producing rice, Raichur is a commercial centre for other agriculture produce such as: cotton, oilseeds, sesame, sorghum, pulses, chillies, groundnut and soap.

The Karnataka power corporation has a Thermal power plant which generates electricity. Raichur Thermal Power Station comprises of eight power generating units, six units of 210 MW and two units of 110 MW. Raichur Thermal Power Plant is one of the nation's most efficient power stations.

Raichur District is one of the few places in India where gold resources are present. Hutti Gold Mines are situated in Raichur District, 90 km., away from Raichur city.

TOURISM POTENTIAL

Raichur city, being the headquarter of Raichur District benefits from the tourism attractions that are in-and-around the District. Because of its considerable antiquity, Raichur district has many places of tourism interest. Brief notes for some of the important places of tourism are presented below.

Raichur Hill Fort

The Raichur fort (Plate 2.1) has a great importance since the past. It is surrounded on three sides with double rows of massive low walls of circuit. The internal wall is made from large blocks of beautifully fitted stones and cementious material. It is said to be made by the Hindus in accordance to the Kannada inscriptions of 1294 A.D. The external wall was built comparatively from rough stone masonry by Muslims.

The external walls of the hill fort of Raichur have five gateways: *(i)* Doddi Darwaza at southeast, *(ii)* Khandak Darwaza at south, *(iii)* Kati Darwaza at east, *(iv)* Naurang Darwaza at north, and *(v)* Mecca Darwaza at west. The internal walls have two gateways: *(i)* Sikandari Darwaza at the east, and *(ii)* Sailani Darwaza at the west.

The Tomb of Pir Sailani Shah

The Tomb of the Muslim Saint, Pir Sailani Shah is also one of the important places of interests in Raichur District. It has fascinating and attractive structure of Bijapur style. It consists of a tiny rectangular entrance with one-arched outlet in every face. The arches are rested on a tiny stone pillars engraved in fashion of Chalukyan. It is loaded with an attractive narrow-necked set of dome on an oblique row of ornaments and lotus petals.

Jamia Masjid

The Fort Jamia Masjid is an attractive mosque structure of two entrances, one in the east and the other in the south. The eastern entrance of the mosque is crowned with three tiny domes, one circular dome in the middle and other two, which are pyramidal. At the left side of this entrance is a deep well of significant dimensions and masonry stonewalls. The south entrance of the mosque is supported with six gigantic stone pillars of Chalukyan style, which is decorated in the middle portions and with angular capitals and square bases. On the opposite side of this entrance is a courtyard cemetery, which contains the graves of the dynasty members of Adil Shahi.

Hindu Palace

Parallel to the Fort Jami Masjid is the archaic Hindu Palace. This palace is an original one with minimal remains as of today, except for the imposing entrance at the side of the jail and the old-walled enclosure. The same jail has been partly altered to suit the necessities of the modern times. Enough care has been taken not to deprive the ancient palace its primitive interest and grandeur.[50]

Venkatapur

Venkatapur village, located in Lingsugur Taluk, has two hills at its south-end. The village contains 45 cairns along its skirt. Another group of cairns with double rings are found at western side of the village.[50]

Bichal

Bichal of Raichur taluk, is known for the Matha of Sri Saviradevaru Channaveera Shivacharya Swami.

Deodurg

Deodurg located about 55 km., west of Raichur, was formerly a stronghold of Bidar chieftains and has an old fort. Nearby, there is a hill, which contains talc.

Devarbhupur

Devarbhupur of Lingsugur taluk, is known for its Amareshwara temple and jaggery trade. The temple is beautifully situated amidst hillocks, with greenery around. Under the auspices of this temple, annually a big jatara (festival) takes place in the month of Phalguna.

Devarsugur

Devarsugur of Raichur taluk is located on the right bank of the Krishna River. This place is known for Sugureshwara or Veerabhadra temple. The annual jatara (festival) of this temple, held in the month of Margashira, attracts a large number of people.

Gabbur

Gabbur of Deodurg taluk, has several old temples and inscriptions. In the earlier days, it was an important seat of education and was known as Gopuragrama. The most important of the temples are those of Basaveshwara, Ishwara, Bangara Basappa and Hanuman. In addition to these, there are several ruined temples, mathas, a few cisterns and a gateway called the Chandi-gage with a temple on either side of it. The Male-Shankara temple is built of rough grey stone and has a high plinth. There are two inscriptional tablets at the northern and western entrances and there is a large cistern in front of the temple.

According to an inscription dated 1109 A.D., belonging to the reign of Vikramaditya VI of the Chalukyas of Kalyana, but originally belonging to a Jain Temple at Gabbur, the place (then called Gobbur or Hiriya Gobbur) was an agrahara town in the 12th century A.D. The same record states that it had also a Jain temple called Brahma-Jinalaya or Nagara-Jinalaya.

Gandhal

Gandhal, in Raichur taluk, which is situated about 32 km., south of Raichur, has a well known temple of Panchamukhi Prana Devaru (Hanuman with five faces) on a hillock.

Hutti

Hutti of Lingsugur taluk located 18 km., from Lingsugur, is well known for its gold mines.

Jaladurga

Jaladurga, in Lingsugur taluk, is an island fort situated picturesquely in the Krishna River. This island fort, located 13 km., from Lingsugur, was an important fort of the Adil Shahs of Bijapur, and Meadows Taylor has given a fine description of it in his book, Noble Queen (1874).

Kallur

Kallur, in Manvi taluk, is a large village located about 21 km., from Raichur. The present village is transformed with modern growth, is surrounded by an old wall. The five gates appear have been constructed during the Muslim period. Two of them are not in use and have no names. The other three are called after the towns to which they lead, *(i)* Manvi Darwaza, *(ii)* Kalmala Darwaza and *(iii)* Raichur Darwaza.

There are six temples in and around the village. Of these Markandeshwara temple is the oldest one and its hall is adorned with pillars made of black polished stone with beautiful carvings on them. A number of inscriptions have been found in this village, most of them belonging to the period of the Chalukyas of Kalyana.

Kavital

Kavital, in Manvi taluk, is a village, situated on the Raichur-Lingsugur road, about 64 km., from Raichur. There is a hillock to the south-west of village which has several natural caverns. Along the slopes of the hill, artefacts, iron slag and pieces of ancient pottery were found. To the west of the village is an ash-mound on the top of which, in later times, a temple has been built. The ash-mound marks the site of an old smelting factory. There is an interesting medieval temple in the village, called Tryambakeshwara temple, which has three shrines, two of which contain lingas. There are two Kannada inscriptions in the temple and a beautiful image of Mahishasuramardini in one of the two niches in its western wall.

Korva (Kolan) (Naradagadde)

Korva of Raichur taluk, is a beautiful island surrounded by Krishna River. This place is located 29 km., north-east of Raichur. It is looked upon as a holy place and is popularly known as Naradagadde, where sage Narada is said to have performed penance.

It has a temple dedicated to Narada, a famous Veerashaiva Matha, the samadhi of Vairagya Channabasavaswami who lived about four centuries ago and was well known for his mystic wisdom, a Shivayoga Peetha and a Basavanna temple. The annual jatara (festival) at this place attracts large number of people and a cattle fair is also held at the same time.

Koormagadde

Just near Naradagadde, there is Koormagadde (Kurumakshetra or Kuravakala) which has a Dattatreya Peetha and the samadhi of Sripadavallabha Swami. It is said to be the original place of Dattatreya. It has a temple dedicated to him, which is visited by devotees from far and near.

Kotekal

Kotekal, in Manvi taluk, is situated on the Raichur-Lingsugur road, about 18 km., from Lingsugur. The village has two hillocks, each having a fort at its top. Along the slopes of these hillocks several artefacts, iron-slags and gold-crushers, belonging to the prehistoric period were found.

Lingsugur

Lingsugur, the taluk head quarters is an important commercial centre. Neolithic implements like: stone axes, hammers, flakes and cores and plain pottery were discovered here.

Manvi

Manvi, is the taluk headquarters and is the centre for developmental activities under the Tungabhadra Project. It has a well-known temple of Jagannathaswami and an old fort which is in ruins now.

Maski

Maski, in Lingsugur taluk, situated 27 km., south-east of Lingsugur on the right bank of Maski Nala a tributary of the Tungabhadra, is highly significant from the points of view of prehistory and protohistory. Maski has proved to be one of the most important prehistoric sites in the district. As early as 1888, Bruce Foote, who collected various kinds of Neolithic implements and artefacts, which are now exhibited in the prehistoric section of the Madras museum.

Matmari

Matmari of Raichur taluk, is looked upon as a holy place. It has a temple dedicated to Veerabhadra and the well-known Matha of Sri Saviradevaru Channaveera Shivacharya Swami is located nearby.

Mudgal

Mudgal of Lingsugur taluk, is one of the most important places of historical interest in the district. The fort at Mudgal is constructed taking the advantage of a hillock. On top of the hillock they built houses of royalty and a wall with bastions. The outer fortifications of Mudgal cover an area of half a square mile. The outer fort has a wide moat, which is filled with water. The width of the moat varies, being as much as 50 yards (46 m) at several places. Behind the moat, there is a scarp with a row of bastions and after that, a narrow covered passage and adjoining it the counter scarp with very massive bastions. From the arrangement of the existing fort, it is apparent that the fort was rebuilt after the inventions of guns. The courses of masonry at several places are of Hindu style, but the arch-shaped parapet is of Muslim design. The moat and the row of bastions together offer a pleasing view.

The Bala Hisar or citadel is built at the top of the hillock and commands a good view of the interior of the fort as well as that of the surround country. The view gives a good idea of the extent of the fort and the large garrison, which could be accommodated therein. There are several natural depressions in the rock above, which were utilized for storing water. Bastions and walls are built at different points for the defence of the buildings of the Bala Hisar. In the middle also, there is a large bastion, round in form. The hill near this bastion rises in the form of a spur and is detached from the lower parts of the hill by a ravine. There are some natural caverns below the Nauras Burj. The fort is defended towards the south-west by a range of hills. In the western part of the fort is a large cistern called the Hikrani Baoli – about 140 yards (130 m) in length and 40 to 50 yards (46 m) in breadth.

Mudval

Mudval, in Lingsugur taluk, is situated 19 km., from Lingsugur. The village has a stone-wall which shows that it was of considerable importance at some time. This is one of the important pre-historic sites of the district. Artefacts were found on the slopes of the hill about a mile and a half to the west of the village. Gold crushers and iron slags were found in abundance near this place.

Mukkunda

Mukkunda, in Sindhanur taluk, is situated on the bank of the Tungabhadra, nearby a hill, about 32 km., from Sindhanur. There is an old and large fort on the top of the hill. At the entrance to the village, there is an old temple of Murari, built of stone. An island in the river has the dargah of Gaddikhader Wali, where an annual urs is held, which attracts a large number of people.

Ramagadde

Ramagadde, in Raichur taluk, about 14 miles (23 km.,) north of Raichur, is a beautiful island in the Krishna River. It is looked upon as a holy place. According to a legend, Sri Ramachandra stayed here for a year and consecrated and worshipped a Shivalinga. It has a Veerashaiva Matha.

Roudkunda

Roudkunda, in Sindhanur taluk, is situated 9.7 km., to the east of Gorebal, on the Sindhanur-Gangavati road. The place is one of the important Neolithic sites in the district. To the west of the village, there are two hillocks, one of them has a small fort that belongs to the 16th or 17th century A.D. Artefacts were found in abundance both in the valley between the two hillocks and on the slopes of the hillock having the fort.

Somalpur

Somalpur, in Sindhanur taluk, about 23 km., from Sindhanur, is well known for its Ambadevi temple, situated at the foot of a hill, where annually a fair takes place in the month of Pushya, which is largely attended.

Malladagudda

Malladagudda is situated about 26 km., from Manvi taluk. There are several caves in the Hill apart from the temples of Veerabhadra, Venkateswar and Devi.

A CITIZENS' VIEW OF RAICHUR CITY

A city belongs to the people who live in it. Thus, it's essential to get to know what the people feel about their city, what issues matter to them and

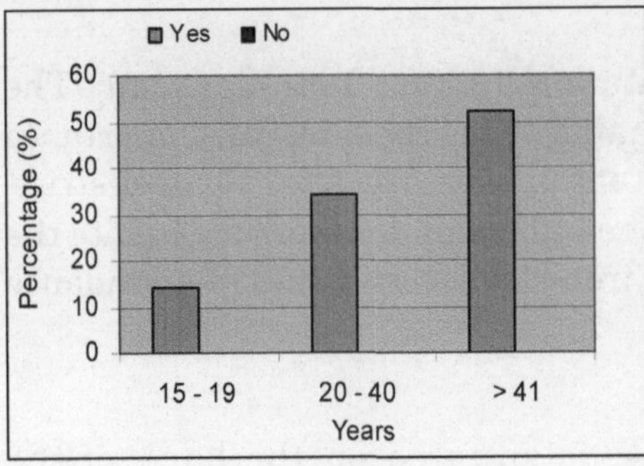

(a) Is Raichur a city?

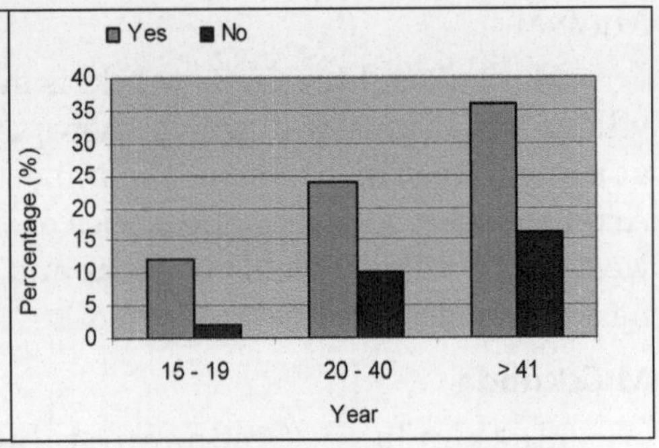

(b) Are you happy seeing Raichur transform into a city?

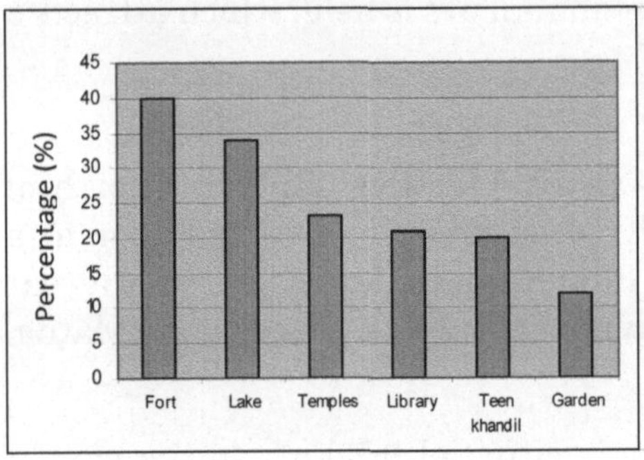

(c) Top three things Raichur is known for?

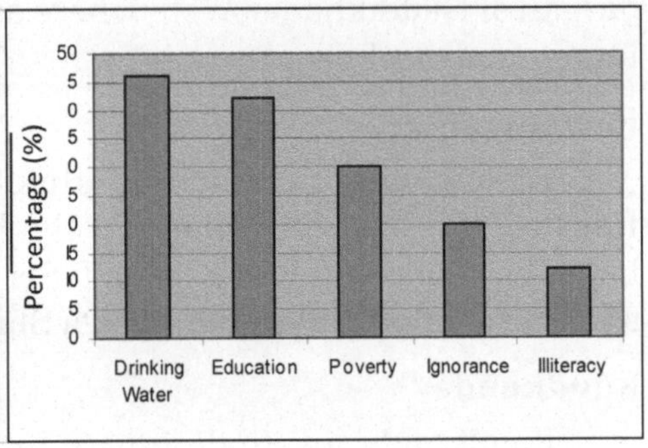

(d) Top three critical issues that Raichur is facing today?

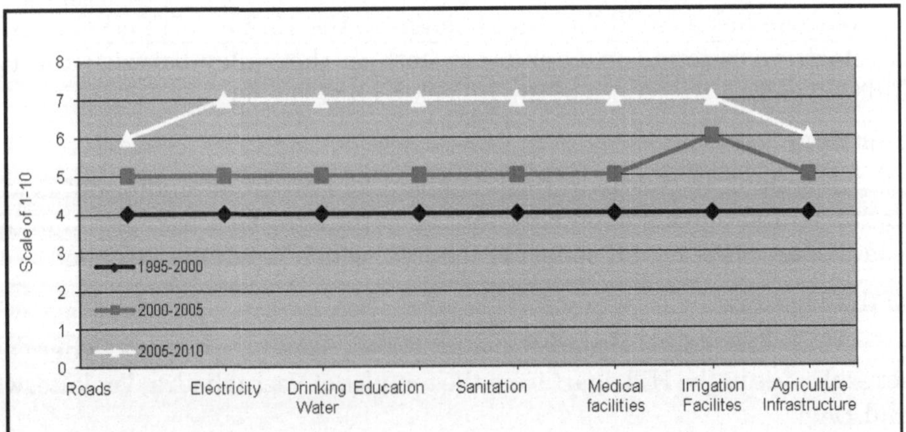

Ranking of progress achieved by Raichur in the various sectors in last 15 years.

Fig. 2.6: People's View on the Various aspects of Raichur

their view about the city. In this context, a questionnaire study has been done to bring forth the view of Raichur residents about their city.

The questionnaire was presented to the residents, who were chosen to represent the various age groups of:

1. Less than 15 to 19 years.
2. Between 20 to 40 years.
3. Greater than 40 years.

The survey has yielded some interesting results (Figure 2.6). Raichur, like most of the cities is agrarian and rural in nature. The transition of a city from rural to urban is often slow and appears natural for the residents. In other words, the transition doesn't catch them as surprise. But in some cases, it can be very dynamic and rapid, which makes people sit-up and think that they are caught in the process of urbanization. In this case, the residents find it difficult to accept the new environment. In both the cases, once the residents are aware that they are in a city, they start demanding the services and utilities that a city deserves. Across the various age groups, all the sample residents are aware that Raichur is a city. This comes as a surprise considering that Raichur got the status of a city only a decade ago. And 72 per cent of the residents are happy to see the transformation of Raichur as city.

The residents unanimously consider that Raichur is famous for cotton, milk and paddy. Raichur fort, lake (am-talab), and temples are on the top list of things that the residents think Raichur is known.

Drinking water, education and poverty are the issues that are very critical for the residents and hence, these areas deserve priority in the development planning for Raichur.

In the last 15 years, the residents found 75 per cent improvement in the areas of drinking water, irrigation, education, power supply, sanitation and medical facilities. Roads and agriculture are put on the average scale and hence, these areas need focus in the development planning of Raichur city.

SUMMARY

Raichur has most of the potential qualities of expanding into a major sprawl because of its agriculture, commerce, tourism potential and infrastructure facilities.

Several factors have contributed for this stature such as: its strategic geographic location, being the headquarter of the district and its proximity to Hyderabad, the state capital of Andhra Pradesh.

The hot climate and the rocky mountains spread in-and-around Raichur might have had an impact on the congested growth of the city.

3

ASSESSING THE LAND-USE, LAND-COVER PATTERN USING GIS AND REMOTE SENSING

INTRODUCTION

As population increases, so does the need for new housing, schools, transportation, and other civic amenities. This had been earlier considered as urbanization, a development that was considered as advancement. But soon the burgeoning population and industrial growth has imposed such huge demands for infrastructure that it has changed the very face of urban development to that of urban sprawl.

Sprawl has been criticized for eliminating agricultural lands, spoiling water quality, and causing air pollution.[16] Symmetrical growth of urban centres consumes agricultural land adjacent to these, resulting in lower agricultural productivity. Besides taxing the groundwater resources available for an urban centre, an increase in the paved area severely reduces the groundwater recharge potential, leading to situations which may truly be potential catastrophes.[17]

In recent years, understanding the dynamics of sprawl, quantifying them and sub-sequently predicting the same for a future period has attracted significant interest of researchers. Measurement of these traits and additional attributes are used to develop standardized indices of sprawl development. Some researchers, have employed an array of indicators, including land-use conversion, population change, traffic and vehicles, miles travelled, energy consumption, and fiscal measures.[29] Other researchers focused on measuring sprawl through the use of population data and detailed land-use and land-cover pattern.[58, 65] The physical expressions and patterns of sprawl on landscapes can be detected, mapped, and analyzed using remote sensing and GIS (Geographical Information System) technologies.[31, 33, 59, 60, 62, 63, 64, 67, 68] Also there are dedicated software programmes developed for simulating urban sprawl: NAUTILUS[32] and EMPACT.[66]

In the present study, an attempt has been made to study the impact of growing urbanization on the land-use and land-cover pattern of Raichur city. This city is still young but already there are indicators which are pointing towards the rampant and uncontrolled growth. In view of this, the present study assumes significance in understanding the growth pattern of the city and cause the impetus required for curbing the sprawl.

DATASETS AND METHODS

For studying the temporal changes in land-use, land-cover pattern of Raichur city, Survey of India (SOI) toposheets (Figure 3.1) and satellite imagery for different periods of time were procured from NRSC (National Remote Sensing Centre, Hyderabad) (Table 3.1).

Table 3.1: Satellite Imagery Procured from National Remote Sensing Centre

Satellite	Sensor	Path and Row	Date of Acquisition	Spatial Resolution
IRS 1C	LISS 3	099-061	17-MAR-98	23.5 m
IRS 1D	LISS 3	099-061	16-FEB-03	23.5 m
IRS P6	LISS 4	102-076	07-MAR-09	5.8 m

SOI toposheets 56 H/7/SW, 56 H/7/SE, 56 H/8/NW and 56 H/8/NE on 1:25000 scale were used as base maps. The major portion of Raichur city municipal limit is covered within the extents of toposheet No: 56 H/8/NW. However, for studying the dynamics of urban sprawl and its impact on the surrounding environs and the nearby villages, an area extent of 260 sq km., around the present core urban area has been considered for the study (Figure 3.1).

The satellite imagery was processed using image processing software - ERDAS Imagine 8.6. LISS-III and IV satellite imagery were imported and saved with the combination of 2 (red), 3 (blue) and 4 (green). The imagery was geo-referenced based on the features of SOI topomap.

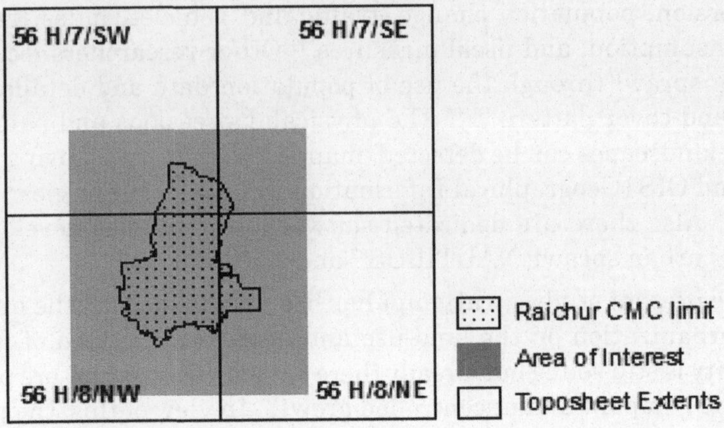

Fig. 3.1: Incidence of Raichur CMC Limit and the Area of Interest on Survey of India Topomaps

Automated and supervised (software-based) classification had disadvantages considering the wide range of spectral signatures overlapping diverse land-use categories of scrubs, plantations, rocky outcrops, stony waste and settlements. Hence, the imagery were classified by means of visual interpretation and extensive ground truthing.

The land-use, land-cover mapping and statistical analyses were done using an add-on ArcGIS extension suite – *Graphics and Shapes.*[61] *MS Excel 2000* was used to prepare the graph charts.

RESULTS AND DISCUSSION

Land-use and land-cover pattern during the year 2009 indicates agriculture as the major land-use with 115.5 sq km., 46 per cent of the total land-use. Stony waste, stone quarries and the dried-up water resources span about 73 sq km., (29%) while settlements occupied 19 sq km. 7.7 per cent of the land-use and land-cover (Figure 3.2).

The Raichur municipal limit is spread over 57 sq km., with residential settlements (19.33 sq km.,) as predominant land-use, followed by transportation (9.13 sq km.,) and industrial use (6.5 sq km.,) (Figure 3.3).

Temporal Change Analysis

- *Settlements*: The core of Raichur city, the densest built-up area, is spread within a radius of 3 km., (Figure 3.2). The remaining settlements are strewn sporadically around this core up to a distance of 10 km.

Interestingly no new patches of settlements were observed since 1982. The city had been sprawling outwards from the core area and the peripheral nuclear patches of settlements. Between 1982 and 1998, there was three

Fig. 3.2: Land-use, Land-cover Map of Raichur City, 2009. The Dotted Circle Represents the Core of Raichur City – The Densest Built-up Area

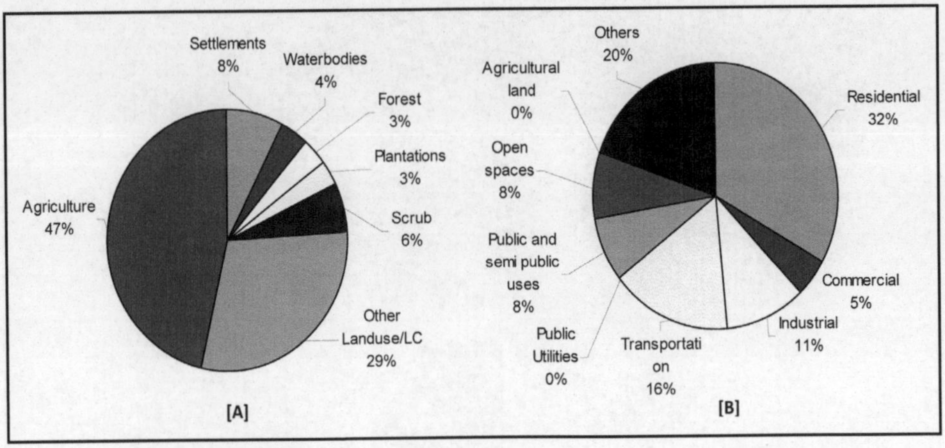

Fig. 3.3: The Pattern of Land-use, Land-cover during 2009: (A) Raichur and its Surroundings (B) within the Limits of Raichur City

times increase in the core and fringe areas. Between 1998 and 2002, the growth at the core remained stable while the fringes have spread by 20 per cent more. During the period, 2002 and 2009, the core as well as fringes saw a growth of 1.5 times (Figure 3.4 and 3.5).

Linear regression analysis indicates that these settlements could expand upto 24 sq km., an increase of nearly 35 per cent by the year 2020.

Demographic profile of Raichur indicates that the decadal growth rate during 1981-91 and 1991-2001, has come down by 8.6 times and the population density has increased but only marginally (Figure 3.6). The stable population with an increase in the built-up area indicates that the city is growing horizontally.

- *Water Resources:* The water resources are heavily dependent on the rainfall and the water supply from the two rivers – Krishna and Tungabadra. Thus, the extent of agriculture cultivation is directly correlated with the spread of water resources. Thus, 2002 had better water resources spread and hence than any other year.
- *Plantations*: There was no significant change in the spread of plantations between 1982-1998 and 2002. In 2009, an increase of 2.5 per cent was noticed. The lack of good rains impacted the cultivation of agriculture. The dried-up water bodies and some agriculture fields were converted to plantations and hence the marginal increase in the increase of plantations during 2009.

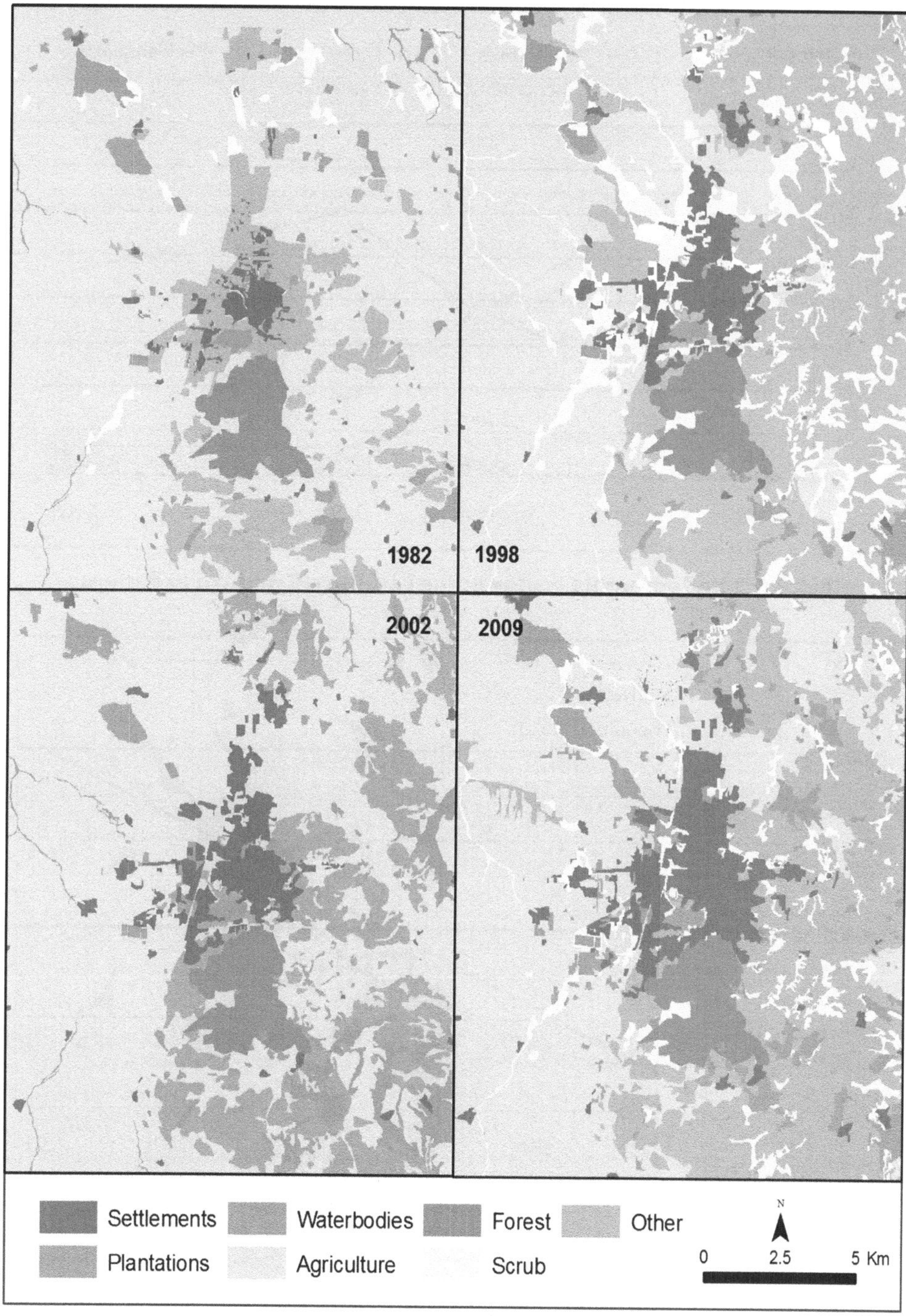

Fig. 3.4: Temporal Changes in the Land-use/Land-cover Pattern for Raichur City

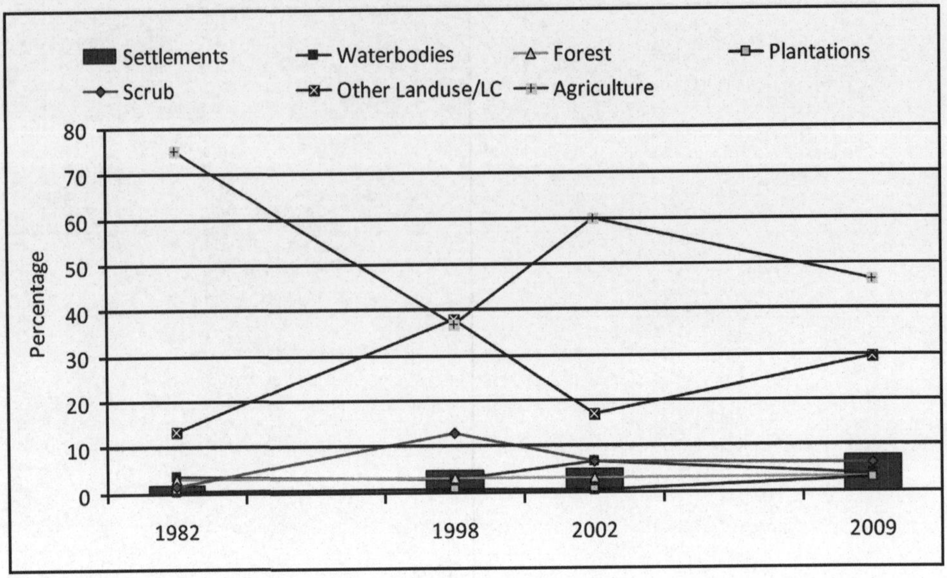

Fig. 3.5: The Temporal Change in the Land-use /Land-cover Pattern

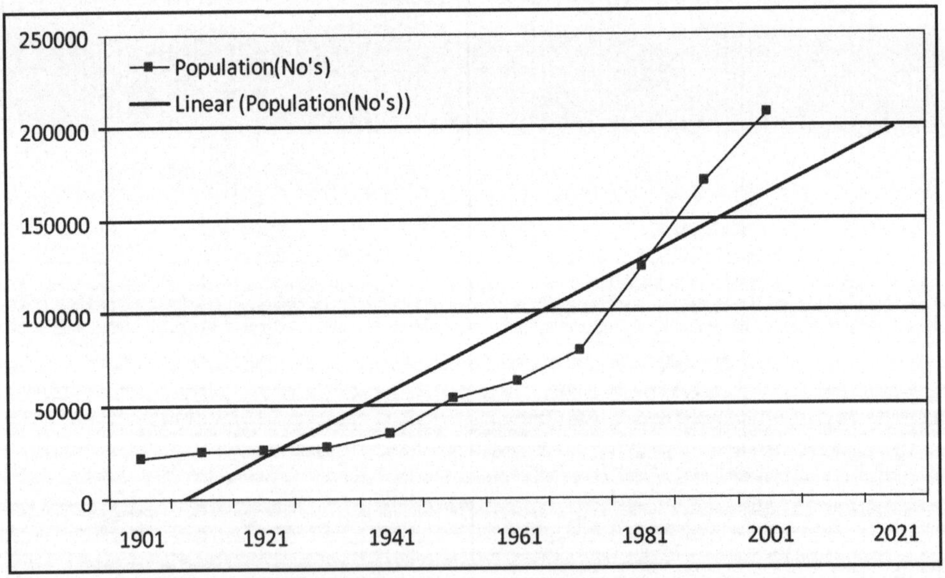

Fig. 3.6: Population Growth of Raichur.[56]
The Population has been Projected for the Years 2011 and 2021

- *Scrubs:* During the year 1982 and 1998 (Figure 3.5), there was 6 times increase, while it reduced by half in 2002. During the year 2002 and 2009, there had been no significant change in the total area occupied by scrubs.

- *Agriculture:* As mentioned earlier, agriculture is directly dependent on the extent of water resources spread. In Raichur, 47 per cent of the agricultural land is irrigated by means of canals, tanks and lift irrigation, the sources which are directly dependent on the rainfall. While the remaining 53 per cent is irrigated by means of bore wells and dug wells (Figure 3.7).

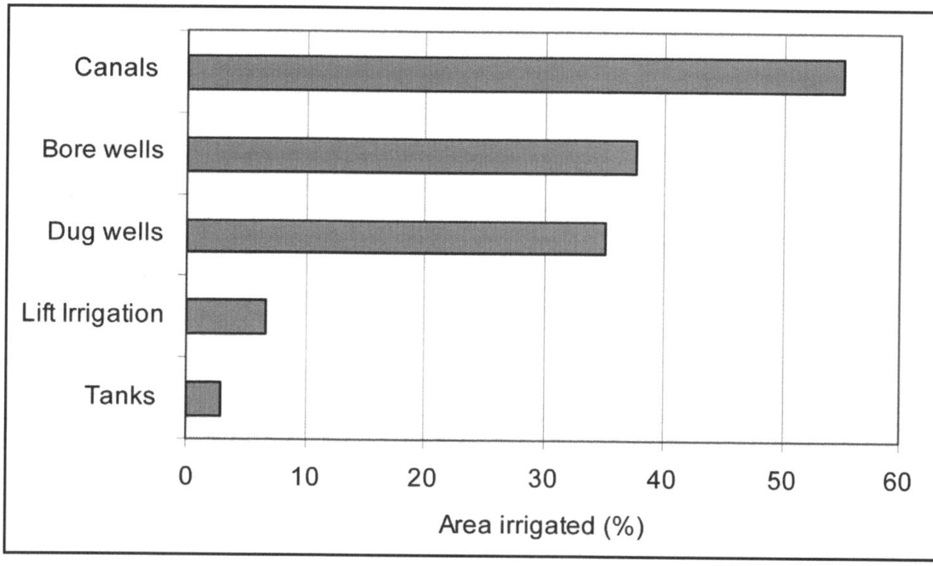

Fig. 3.7: The Typical Pattern of the Land Irrigated through Various Sources

Earlier, the farmers cultivated oil seed as the main crop. Two decades ago, they switched to growing Sona Masoori variety of rice as the main crop. Cotton is grown in the areas where little or no irrigation is available.

Linear regression analysis indicates that by 2020, nearly, 29 per cent of the agriculture land would be converted to settlements. Thus, agriculture and settlements would share almost equal area by 2020.

- *Forest:* There's only one patch of forest land, measuring 8.2 sq km., that too quite close to the core of Raichur city. And surprisingly, since last 29 years there had been neither any encroachment nor there had been any additions to this category.

SUMMARY

The present agrarian land-use of Raichur is under imminent threat from the rapid and burgeoning urbanization. Considering the present trend, by 2020, nearly 29 per cent of the agriculture land would be converted to settlements. Moreover, the agriculture in this region depends on both the surface and ground water resources. The increasing urbanization would increase the demand of ground water which in turn would further impact the agriculture. Thus, it's imperative to formulate appropriate measures to check the haphazard growth of urbanization.

4

DEMOGRAPHY AND SOCIO-ECONOMIC INDICATORS

INTRODUCTION

Raichur is one of the rapidly growing cities in the state of Karnataka. It is an important commercial and industrial centre and famous for trading cotton, paddy and other agricultural produce. The irrigation facilities under Tungabhadra canal have stabilized the agriculture prosperity, catalysing the prospects of setting up agro-based industries such as: rice and oil mills. Apart from these, there is immense scope for the development of medium and small scale industries.

DEMOGRAPHIC PROFILE

As of 2001 India census, Raichur city had a population of 2,07,421; males were 51 per cent of the population and females 49 per cent (Table 4.1). The total population of Raichur constitutes 4 per cent of Karnataka state's total population and 0.02 per cent of the total India population. As the population of Raichur exceeds one lakh, it has been categorised as Class I town and a city (Table 4.2).

The ward-wise population distribution indicates (Figure 4.1) that the most populated wards are 3, 4, 8, 13, 22, 29, 33, 35, and 36 in the range of 7000 and 9407; the highest population being 9407, with the male population of 4853 and female population of 4554 in ward 30.

The wards 3, 22, 29, and 35 have the highest number of households in the range of 1501 to 2000 (Figure 4.1).

Table 4.1: Population, Decadal Growth Rate, Sex Ratio and Density – States/ Union Territories and Districts[53]

India and State/ Union Territory* /District/City	Population 2001			Decadal Growth Rate		Sex Ratio	
	Persons	Males	Females	1981-1991	1991-2001	1991	2001
India	1,027,015,247	531,277,078	495,738,169	23.86	21.34	927	933
Karnataka	52,733,958	26,856,343	25,877,615	21.12	17.25	960	965
Raichur District	1,648,212	832,352	815,860	30.53	21.93	979	983
Raichur City	207,421	105,785	101,636	36.72	21.60	943	961

Table 4.2: Classification Criteria of Towns and Cities[53]

Classification	Population Size
Class I towns*	100,000 and above
Class II towns	50,000 to 99,999
Class III towns	20,000 to 49,999
Class IV towns	10,000 to 19,999
Class V towns	5,000 to 9,999
Class VI towns	Less than 5,000

*The larger size class towns of class-I are referred to as cities

Population Density

Population density of Raichur has increased by 21 per cent between 1991 and 2001.[52] The gross density of the city is 96 persons per ha. The desirable gross density is 100 persons per ha.

Population Growth Rate

Population growth rate (PGR) of Raichur city is comparatively higher than that of Raichur district and Karnataka state (Figure 4.2 and 4.3). The high PGR in the case of Raichur city during the years 1951 and 1981 could be attributed to the re-organization of the state and or the sudden migration of large population due to the irrigation facilities created by the Tungabhadra Irrigation Project. This migrated population constituted of agriculture laborers, workers and staff involved with the irrigation project.

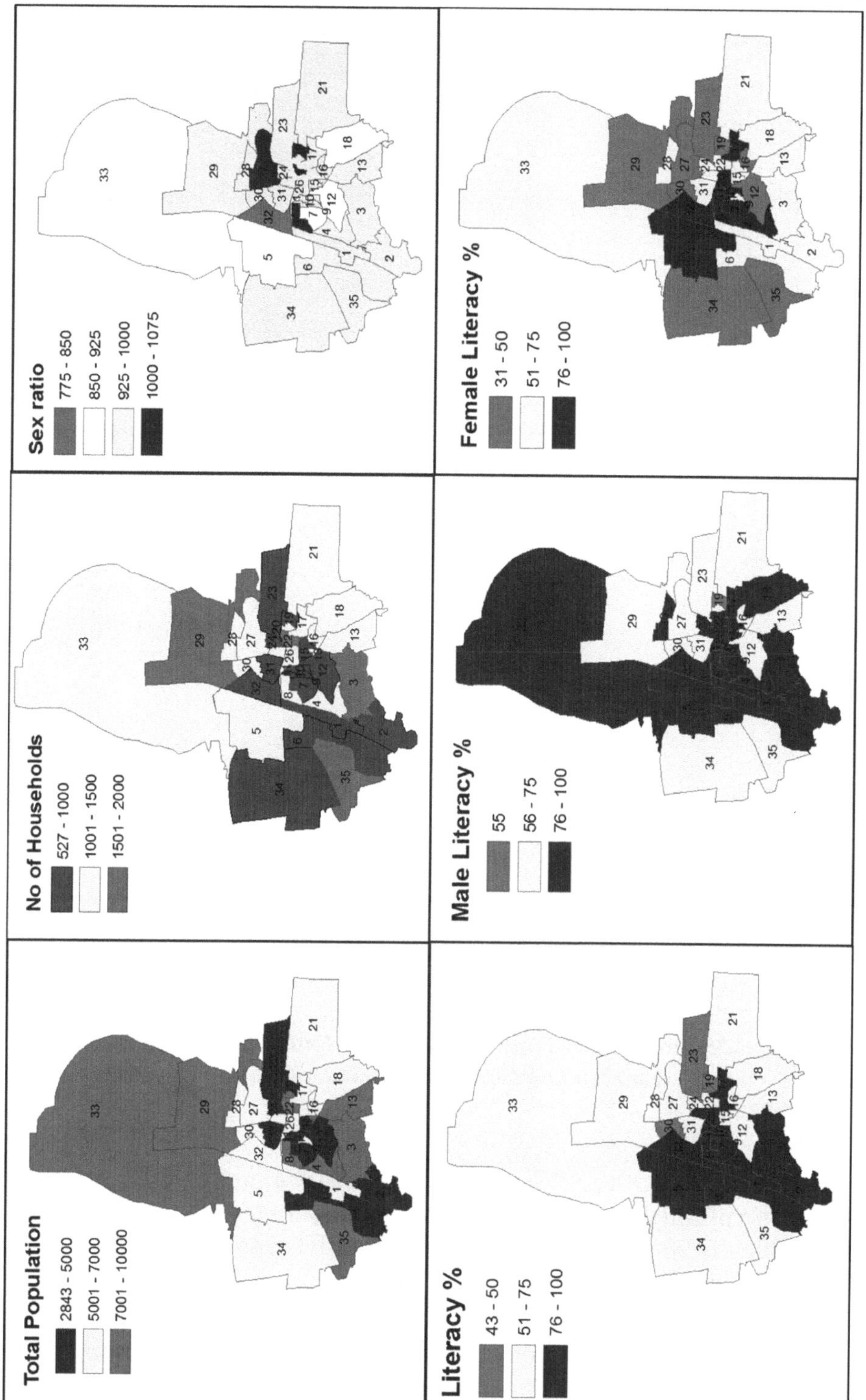

Fig. 4.1: Ward-wise Census Details, 2001 for Raichur City[53]

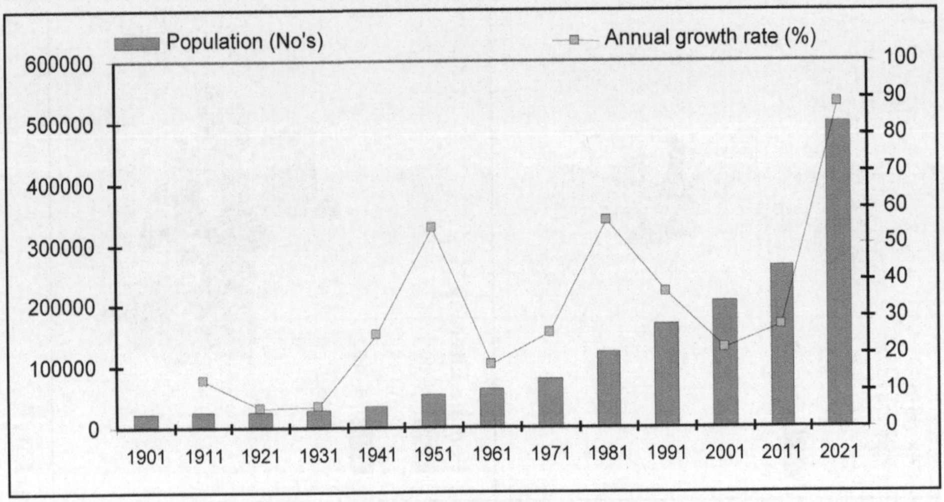

Fig. 4.2: Decadal Census Data for Raichur City[53]

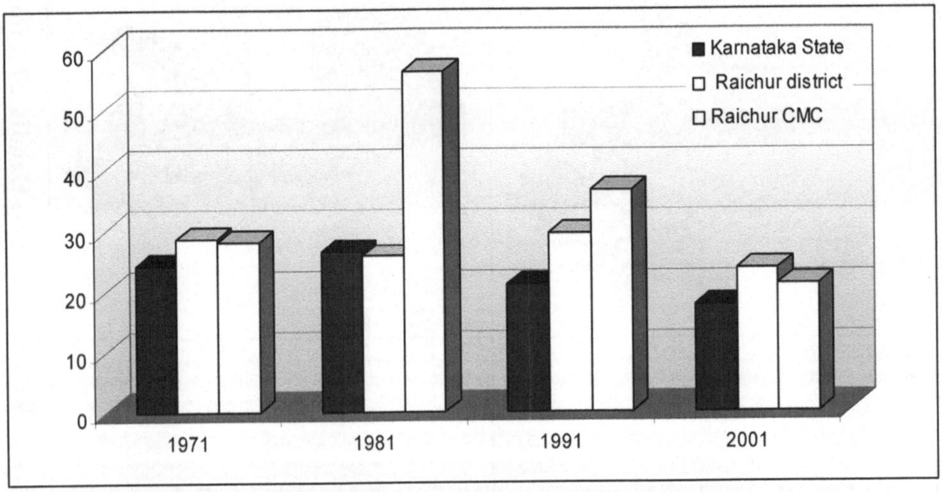

Fig. 4.3: Comparative Population Growth Rate of Raichur City, Raichur District and Karnataka State[53]

Sex Ratio

The average sex ratio of Raichur city is 961 females per 1000 males.[53] The sex ratio of Raichur city is lesser than the average sex ratio of Raichur district which is 983 and is at par with that of Karnataka (965) and India (933) as well (Table 4.1). The sex ratio of Raichur city has improved by 2 per cent between 1991 and 2001; and 4 per cent between 1971 and 2001.

The ward-wise spatial analysis indicates, the highest sex ratio, in the range of 1000-1075 was found in wards 8, 19, 22 and 27 (Figure 4.1).

Literacy Rate

Literacy in India is a key indicator for socio-economic progress (UNESCO). Raichur city has an average literacy rate of 70.4 per cent, much better than the national average of 62 per cent (Table 4.3).

The literacy rate for Raichur city has been 23 per cent better during 1991-2001; and 48 per cent better during 1971-2001.

Table 4.3: Literacy Rate of Raichur City, Raichur District and Karnataka State.[53]

Sl. No.	Decade	Literacy Rate%		
		Raichur City	Raichur District	Karnataka State
1.	1971	22.49	20.20	31.52
2.	1981	45.37	24.92	38.41
3.	1991	47.37	28.59	46.72
4.	2001	70.40	48.80	66.60

In the case of Raichur city, the male literacy is 80 per cent which is far better than the national average of 62 per cent, while the national female literacy rate for Raichur city is 61 per cent, better than the national average of 58 per cent. However, there is a wide gender disparity in the literacy rate in Raichur city (Table 4.4).

The low female literacy is considered to have dramatically negative impact on family planning and population stabilization efforts in India. Several studies have indicated that female literacy as a strong predictor of the use of contraception among married Indian couples, even when women do not otherwise have economic independence.[69] In the case of Raichur, it's a paradox that though the female literacy is very low and the sex ratio is being desirable, the population growth rate has been on the decline since 1981.

Table 4.4: Number of Literates by Sex and Literacy Rates in 1991 and 2001.[53]

State/Union Territory/ District	Literates			Literacy Rate					
				1991			2001		
	Persons	Males	Females	Persons	Males	Females	Persons	Males	Females
Karnataka	30,774,988	17,817,682	12,957,306	56.04	67.26	44.34	67.04	76.29	57.45
Raichur District	683,988	431,738	252,250	34.34	46.75	21.7	49.54	62.02	36.84

The child literacy rates of Raichur are not commensurate with the national mission. By 2001, only 50 per cent of the child populations, in the age group of 0-6, were literate. The urban child literacy fared better over rural with a margin of 25 persons. The gender disparity in child literacy is also very wide as that of adult literacy.

The wards 19, 23, and 30 had lowest literacy rate of less than 50 per cent. The wards, 12, 16, 19, 21, 27, 29, 30, 34, and 35 fared lowest female literacy with less than 50 per cent (Figure 4.1).

Population Projection

Several methods are available in the literature for population projections. Each has certain advantages and disadvantages, and the availability of data and the characteristics of the area under study primarily determine their use.

In the case of Raichur city, a study time frame of 100 years between 1901 till 2001 was used. The decadal population census data was used for estimating the projected population of Raichur CMC for 2011 and 2021 using various methods (Table 4.5).

Trend Analysis Method

A city is assumed to have its own internal dynamics, largely insulated from the external forces. The trends observed in the past are, therefore, taken as indicators of the future. The statistical method of curve fitting belongs to this category. For a steady growth rate, the Linear Projection Method is used. If there is a constant increase in growth rate, the Exponential Curve Projection Method is used. Similarly the Modified Exponential Projection method is used when the town is showing a declining pace of growth rate after approaching an upper capacity limit. This method is more suitable for cities and towns which are not likely to be affected by any foreseen or unexpected drastic change in its growth pattern.

Table 4.5: Projected Population of Raichur City using various Methods[52]

Sl.No.	Method	Projected Population	
		2011	2021
1.	Least Square Trend method	272651	351530
2.	Arithmetical Progression method	252224	306704
3.	Geometrical Method	256829	318006
4.	Incremental Increase Method	247242	287063

Least Square Trend Method

Decade	X (Population)	Y (Population)	Log_{10} Y	X Log_{10} Y	X^2
1981	-1	124762	5.09 61	-5.0961	1
1991	0	170577	5.2319	0	0
2001	+1	207421	5.3168	+5.3168	1
Total	**0**		**15.6448**	**0.2207**	**2**

From the above Table,

$X = 0$, $Log_{10} Y = 15.6448$, $X Log_{10} Y = 0.2207$, $X^2 = 2$

N = no of decades = 3

We have, $Y = n a + X b$

Take log on both sides,

$Log_{10} Y = n Log_{10} a + X Log_{10} b$ —————— (1)

Substitute the values in the equation (1)

$15.6448 = 3 Log_{10} a + (0) Log_{10} b$

$15.6448 = 3 Log_{10} a + 0$

$Log_{10} a = 15.6448/3 = 5.2149$

$\therefore a = \text{antilog } (5.2149)$

$\therefore a = 164021.2$

Multiplying the equation (1) by, X

Then,

$X Log_{10} Y = n X Log_{10} a + X^2 Log_{10} b$ —————— (2)

Substitute the values in the equation (2)

$0.2207 = 3 (0) Log_{10} a + 2 Log_{10} b$

$0.2207 = 0 + 2 Log_{10} b$

$Log_{10} b = 0.2207/2 = 0.11035$

$b = \text{antilog } (0.11035)$

$\therefore b = 1.2893$

To estimate the projected population for the year 2011,

We have,

$Y = ab^2$

$Y_{2011} = 164021.2 \times (1.2893)^2$

$Y_{2011} = 2, 72{,}651.$

To estimate the projected population for the year 2021,

We have,

$Y = ab^3$

$Y_{2011} = 164021.2 \times (1.2893)^3$

$Y_{2011} = 3, 51{,}530.$

Arithmetic Progression

The arithmetic projection method for projecting population assumes that growth in a future period will continue at a constant rate established by past growth.

We have,

$P_t = P_0 (1 + r t)$

Where, P_t = Projected population

P_0 = Present Population

t = Period of projection

r = annual rate of population growth

$P_{2001} = P_{1991} (1 + r t)$

$207421 = 170577 (1 + r t)$

$1 + r t = 207421/170577$

$1 + 10 r = 1.216$

$10 r = 0.216$

$r = 0.216/10$

$r = 0.0216$

$P_{2011} = P_{2001}(1 + r t)$

$= 207421 (1+0.0216 \times 10)$

$P_{2011} = 252224$

$P_{2021} = P_{2011}(1 + r t)$

$= 252224 (1+0.0216 \times 10)$

$P_{2021} = 306704$

Geometric Progression

This method assumes that growth in a future period will continue at a logarithmic rate established by past growth.

We have,

$P_t = P_0 (1 + r)^t$

Where, P_t = Projected population

P_0 = Present population

r = rate of population growth

t = time interval between P_t and P_0

Rate of growth of population 1991-2001

i.e., $r = ((207421 - 170577)/170577) \times 100$

$r = 21.60\%$

Yearly growth rate = 21.60/10 = 2.16% = 0.0216

$P_{2011} = P_{2011} (1 + r)^t$

$= 207421 (1+0.0216)^{10}$

$$= 207421\ (1.\ 0216)^{10}$$

$$= 207421 \times 1.2382$$

$$P_{2011} = 2{,}56{,}829$$

$$P_{2021} = P_{2011}\,(1 + r)^{t}$$

$$= 2{,}56{,}829\ (1{+}0.0216)^{10}$$

$$= 2{,}56{,}829\ (1.\ 0216)^{10}$$

$$= 2{,}56{,}829 \times 1.2382$$

$$P_{2011} = 3{,}18{,}006$$

Incremental Increase Method

Growth rate is assumed to be progressively increasing or decreasing, depending upon whether the average of the incremental increases in the past is positive or negative. The population for a future decade is worked out by adding the mean arithmetic increase to the last known population as in the arithmetic increase method, and to this is added the average of incremental increases, once for first decade, twice for second and so on.

Average increase per decade = 42530

Average incremental increase/decrease = –2709

Population for the decade 2011,

i.e. P_{2011} = 207421 + 42530-2709

P_{2011} = 2,47,242

The projected population for the decade 2021,

i.e., P_{2021} = 247242 + 42530 – 2709

P_{2021} = 2, 87,063

Year	Population	Increase	Incremental Increase	Percentage Increase
1971	79831	–	–	–
1981	124762	44931	–	56.28%
1991	170577	45815	884	36.72%
2001	207421	36844	-8971	21.60%
Total	582591	127590	-8127	114.6%
Average	145648	42530	-2709	38.20%

Induced Rate of Growth

In this case, the population is projected on the basis of the employment opportunities which are likely to grow on the basis of past trends, as well as due to committed proposals and the expected proposals likely to be sanctioned.

In this method there is a need to conduct a close study of the induced activity and the effects that it can cause especially in terms of the secondary and tertiary level of opportunities that it can create and their economic implications. This will also include the additional possibilities of economic activities depending upon the availability of resources within the region. If the feasibility and impact study of the activity to be induced is not done properly this method can lead to absolutely misguiding final figures and create chaos in the actual development process.

The industrial growth centre of Raichur, spanning 818 ha, is located towards north-east of the city local planning area (LPA). An area of 736.3 ha is within LPA and 81.7 ha is outside LPA. The major industrial development activities are taken place in the growth centre, which is outside the LPA.[52]

According to the Master Plan-2021 of Raichur, Surana Industries (P) Ltd., Vishvesvaraya Steel Plant (P) Ltd., and central Power Grid Station are some of the major industries likely to be set up which requires large labour, official staff, and other subsidiary workers are expected to shift their families to Raichur city. This migrant population has been estimated as 1,00,000 persons.

Therefore, using the induced rate of growth, the Raichur population for 2021 has been calculated as a total of 5,00,000.[52]

OCCUPATIONAL STRUCTURE

The occupational structure of the people provides a snapshot of the way of life of the people and their economic and social organization.

Agriculture is the main economic base of Raichur City. Towards west of Raichur city, most of the land comes under irrigation facilities of Tungabhadra command area. In these areas, agriculturists are raising irrigated cotton, paddy, jowar, bajra, groundnut, sunflower, tur and other crops. Towards east of the city, one can find mostly rock outcrops and a few plantations that are irrigated by natural streams and surface water bodies. Because of the predominant paddy cultivation, the town has 3 oil mills and 12 rice mills.

Being the district headquarters, Raichur city has very good commercial and administrative base. Abundant natural resources and infrastructure has induced good trade, commercial, and industrial activities.

Raichur population constitutes of 29 per cent main workers, 1 per cent marginal workers and the remaining 70 per cent are non-workers (Figure 4.4). Agriculture labourers form the single largest entity of occupation followed by cultivators and household industries and services (Figure 4.5).

During the year 1991, a sudden increase in the number of agriculture labours, cultivators and household industries and services was observed. Across the years, notably, the non-workers increased at the rate of 39 per cent during the years 1981-91 and 17 per cent during the years 1991-2001 (Figure 4.6). In general, the percentage of female workers was much less compared to the males.

The occupational structure indicates that the predominant activities of Raichur are the ones which fall in the undefined sector followed by trade and commerce, agriculture labours.

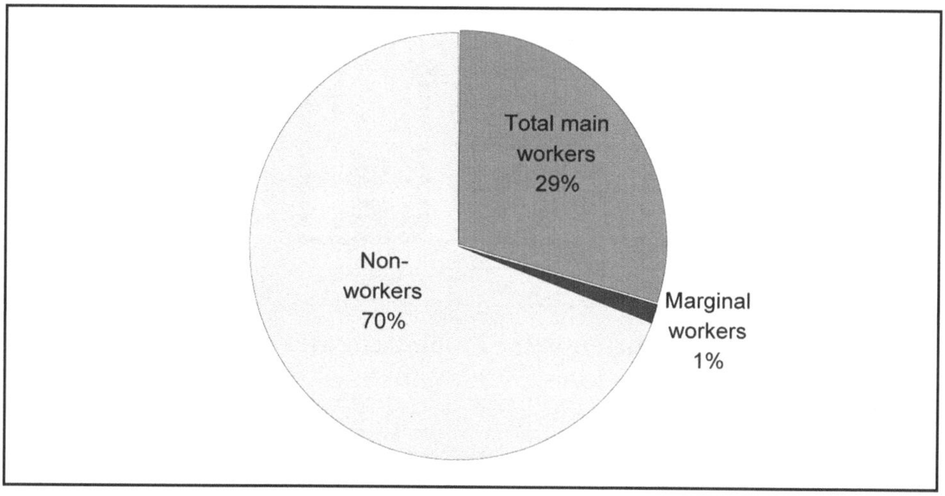

Fig. 4.4: Distribution of Workers and Non-workers in Raichur City in 2001[53]

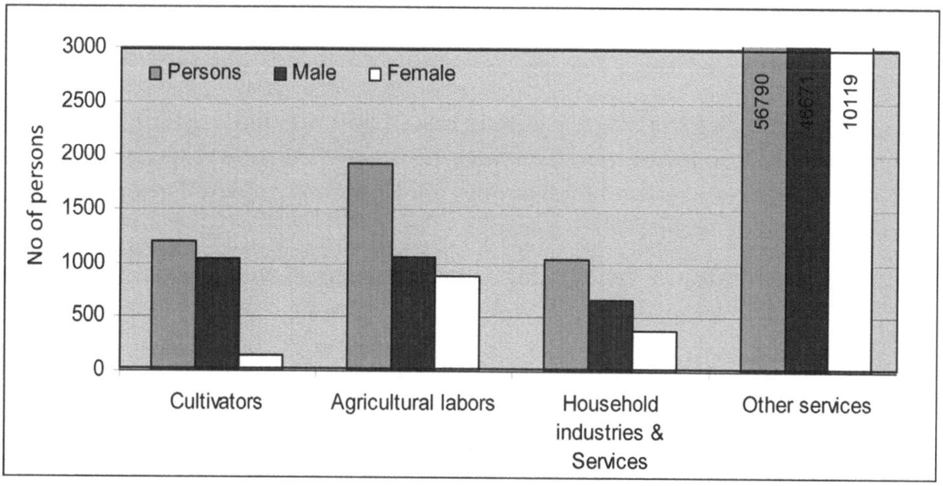

Fig. 4.5: Occupational Structures of the People of Raichur City[53]

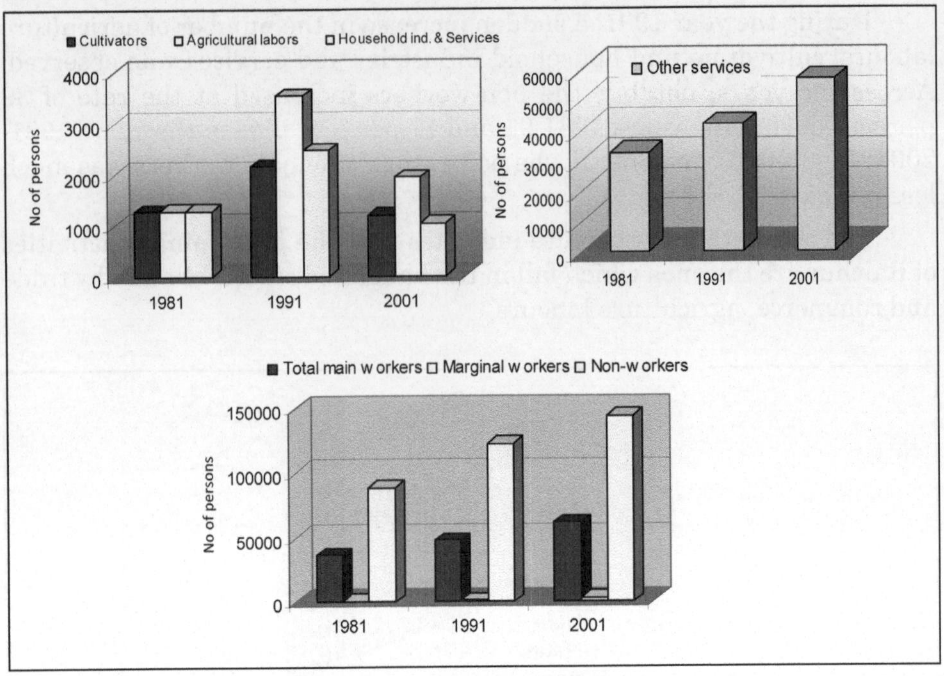

Fig. 4.6: Occupational Structure of the People Across the years for Raichur City[53]

HOUSING

Shelter is a fundamental human need which is essential to protect themselves from the five elements of nature and raise their families and a place to call their own, a house. Yet, a fifth of the world's population is either homeless or live in poor housing conditions. The acute shortage of housing had been a key concern at the international level.

Present Scenario

As per the Census 2001, Raichur has 35850 residential buildings with a shortage of 2230 buildings. Considering a natural growth or an increase of 30 to 35 per cent in the housing, by 2021 for the projected population, it would require at least 3483 buildings (Table 4.6).

The predominant reason for this shortage of housing is affordable availability of developed sites. The developed sites are costly which the lower income groups and economically weaker sections cannot afford. The strict government rules such as: sanction plan criteria favor higher income groups. Because of these reasons, people tend to encroach open lands and build unauthorized structures leading to the formation of slums.

Table 4.6: Decadal House hold Details for Raichur[53]

Decades	No of House Holds	No of Houses	Housing Shortage	HH size
1971	15932	14274	1658	5.56
1961	21795	21549	246	5.79
1991	28291	28084	207	6.07
2001	38080	35850	2230	5.78
2011	50026*	47391	2635	5.23
2021	66129*	62646	3483	6.38

Source: District Census Handbooks (*Projected values)

A majority of the houses of Raichur are very congested with no proper ventilation with mud wall structures. The roofs are made of tin sheets, asbestos sheets and country tiles (Plate 4.1). During summers, it's practically impossible to sit inside these houses. One noticeable feature is that there is severe lack of open spaces. This can be clearly understood from the fact that there are only two parks in the entire city of Raichur.

Various Housing Schemes

Raichur City Municipal Council has created 5 residential layouts under the schemes of Ashraya (2362 plots) and IDSMT (599 plots). Similarly, Urban Development Authority, Raichur is planning to make town extension scheme in Raichur City by purchasing 75 acres of land along the stretches of Siddarampur road, Mantralayam road, and Bolamandoddi road. Plots in these layouts would be provided for the public at reasonable rates. In spite these efforts, the housing scenario of Raichur is still far from the basic housing standards.

The solution for this problem lies in understanding and restructuring the housing policies that can encourage people in building decent homes for themselves. Raichur Urban Development Authority can come forward and provide housing loan assistance. Karnataka Housing Board (KHB), Slum Clearance Board, and Town Planning should prepare their programmes for the construction of houses.

SLUMS

In India, slums have become an integral part of the urbanization.[56] For the formulation of effective and coordinated policy understanding the demography is essential. As part of the 2001 census, formation and identification of slum areas has made it possible for enumeration of various slums across the country, which has been considered as first of its kind across the world.

Plate 4.1 Aerial view of the houses of Raichur (above);

(below) various types of housing roofs: RCC ▭ tin sheets ▭ asbestos sheets

For the purpose of enumeration and demarcation, Census of India (2001) has broadly defined the slum areas as:

(i) All specified areas in a town or city notified as 'Slum' by State/Local Government and UT Administration under any Act including a 'Slum Act'.

(ii) All areas recognized as 'Slum' by State/Local Government and UT Administration, Housing and Slum Boards, which may have not been formally notified as slum under any act.

(iii) A compact area of at least 300 population or about 60-70 households of poorly built congested tenements, in unhygienic environment usually with inadequate infrastructure and lacking in proper sanitary and drinking water facilities.

Raichur city has 55 slums spread across an area of 277 ha, with 18748 households comprising a population of 88530 people. These are spatially spread across the core and the Southeast fringes of the city. More than fifty per cent of the slums are located in six wards: 3, 12, 13, 14, 23 and 29 (Figure 4.7).

Comparing the demography of Raichur, 43 per cent of the Raichur population lives in slums with population density which is 8 times more than that of the rest of India.

A majority of the slum dwellers (83%) occupy state government lands (Figure 4.8). Census of India has categorized slums into notified and non-notified.[56] Slums with households less than 60 are considered as 'non-notified slums'.

LAND VALUE

Land value indicates a combination of factors that drive the urban sprawls. As discussed in Chapter 1, all else being equal, more sprawls occur where land values are lower. (2, 6, 7, and 8)

The spatial analysis of Raichur city indicates that the government price is the highest in ward no 11 for both residential as well as commercial purposes. The land spread in the east, west and north are priced low (Figure 4.9).

The market price is driven by the following guidelines:

1. The core of the city is highly priced the cost of INR 2000/- per sq ft.
2. The areas in the vicinity of slums are priced in the range of INR 400/ - to 500/- per sq ft.
3. The remaining areas are priced in the range of INR 800/- to 1000/- per sq ft.

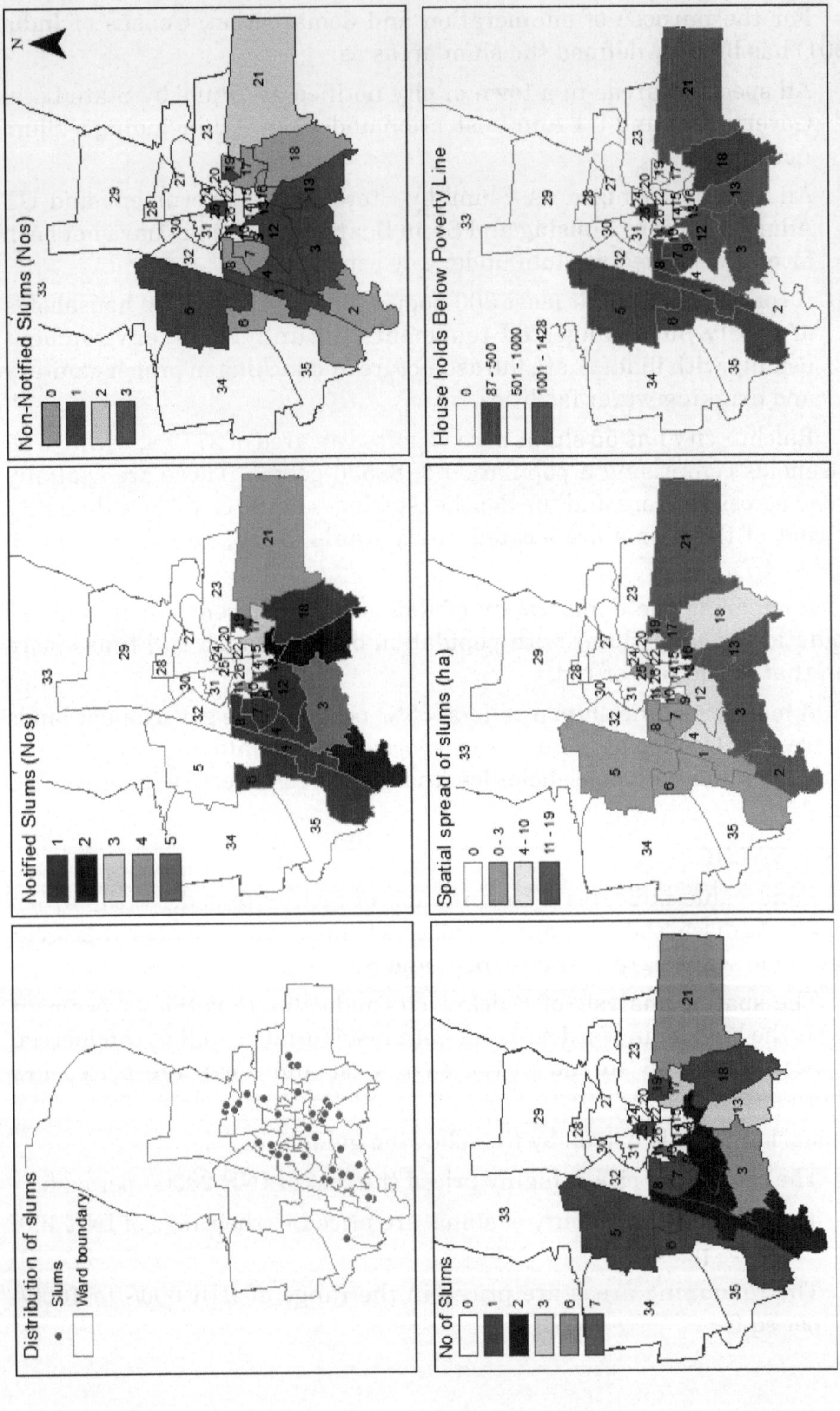

Fig. 4.7: Spatial Analysis of Slums

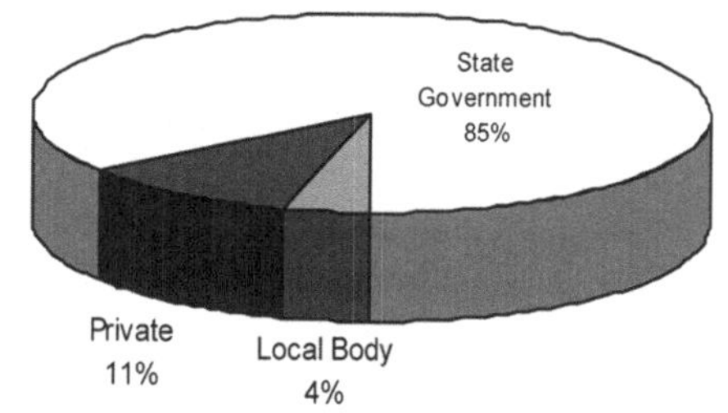

Fig. 4.8 (a): Ownership of the Lands Occupied by Slums

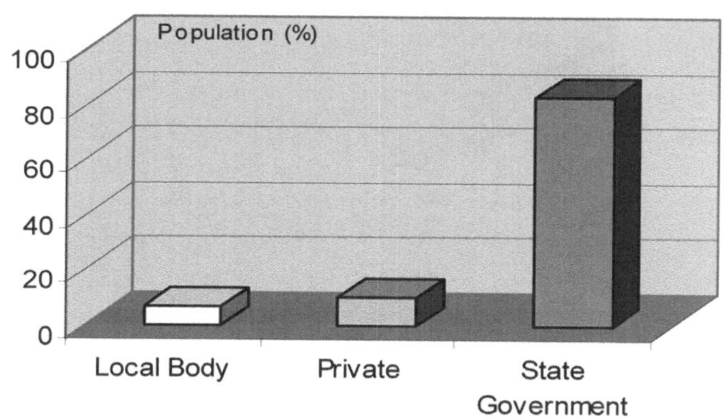

Fig. 4.8 (b): Slum Populations Perched on the Various land Ownerships

Thus, the wards 6, 23, 29, 33, 34 and 35 are priced at INR 800/- to 1000/- per sq ft., and the wards 2, 3, 13 and 18 are priced the lowest in the range of INR 400/- to 500/- per sq ft.

INCOME GROUPS

The income profiles of the people were surveyed to look for the patterns of economic stratification. For the purpose of survey, people earning below INR 8,000/- per month were considered as low income groups, people earning income in the range of INR 8,000/- to 15,000/- per month were considered as medium income groups and above 15,000/- per month as high income groups.

The spatial analysis indicates that Basaveshwara colony, Daddy colony, KEB Quarters, Haji colony, Azad nagar, IB Colony, and Radio Station are the areas with high income group. Most of these areas fall within the radius of core area of Raichur City. A clear and strong delineation could be made between haves and have-nots.

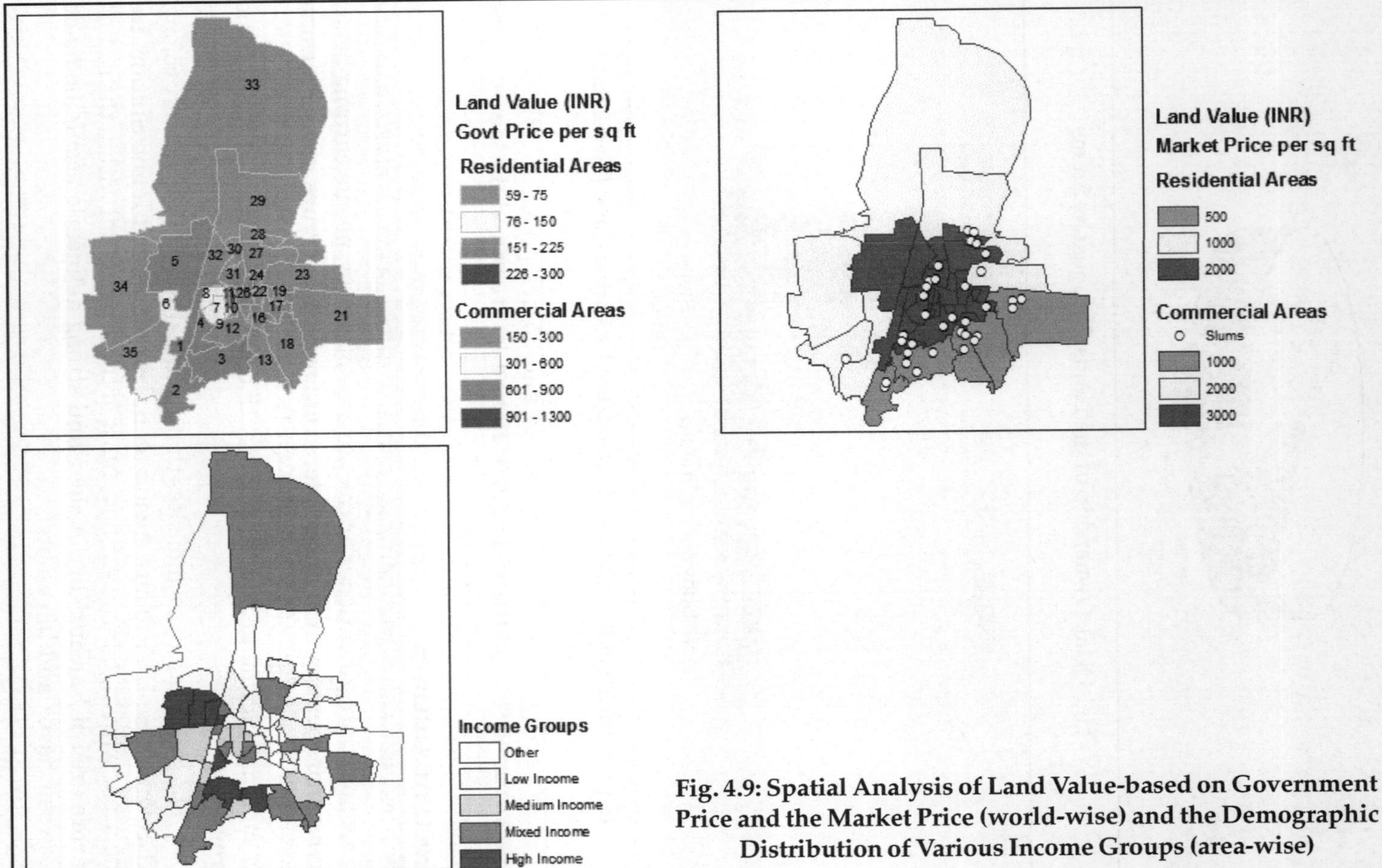

Fig. 4.9: Spatial Analysis of Land Value-based on Government Price and the Market Price (world-wise) and the Demographic Distribution of Various Income Groups (area-wise)

SUMMARY

Raichur is a rapidly growing city of Karnataka with a strong economic base in agriculture, commerce and industry. The economic stratification is clearly marked. Low female literacy, child literacy, slum rehabilitation and large non-worker population is a matter of serious concern that requires to be addressed on priority basis.

5

INFRASTRUCTURE ASSESSMENT OF RAICHUR CITY

INTRODUCTION

Infrastructure consists of the services and facilities necessary for an economy to function.[70] Infrastructure typically refers to the technical structures that support a society, such as: roads, water supply, sewers, power grids, telecommunications, and so forth. Viewed functionally, infrastructure facilitates the production of goods and services. In some contexts, the term may also include basic social services such as: park, open spaces, schools and hospitals.[71]

Urban Infrastructure for Raichur city has been discussed under the categories of social, economic, industrial, power, water supply and sanitation, and transportation and traffic.

SOCIAL INFRASTRUCTURE

Social infrastructure refers to the facilities and mechanisms that ensure education, health care, community development, income distribution, employment and social welfare.

Education

The educational institutions of Raichur city have been surveyed, mapped and presented as Figure 5.1. The spatial pattern indicates that the educational institutions are concentrated in the core of Raichur city.

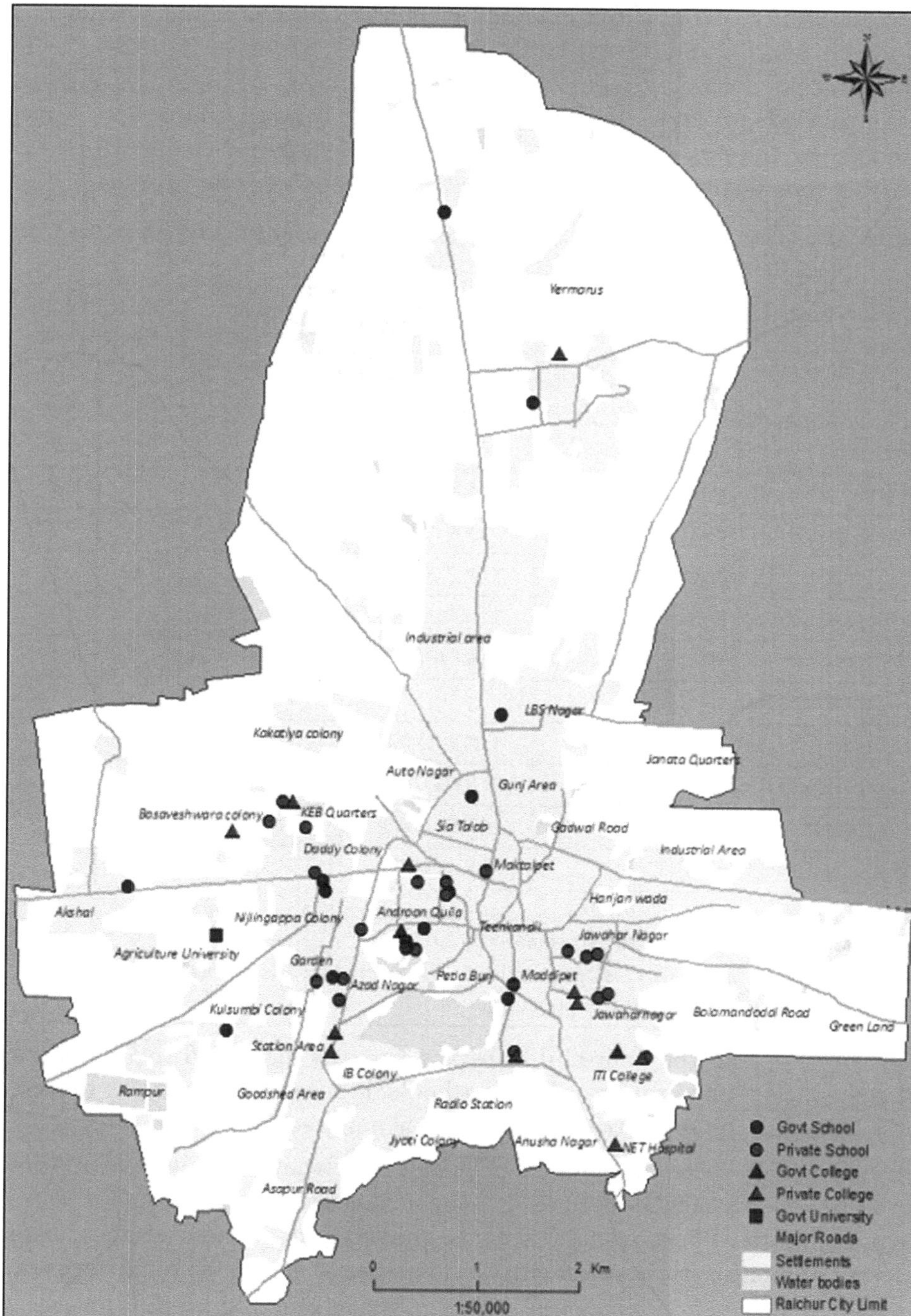

Fig. 5.1: Spatial Distribution of Educational Institutions

Raichur city has 11 pre primary schools, 17 higher primary schools, 7 high schools, 6 Pre-University Course colleges, 4 degree colleges, 2 ITI colleges, 3 polytechnic colleges, 3 Engineering Colleges, 2 Pharmacy Colleges, 2 Dental Colleges and 2 Medical Colleges (Table 5.1 and Figure 5.2). Apart from these, the city also has *University of Agricultural Sciences, Raichur* with various degree, diploma and agricultural engineering courses.

Table 5.1: The Existing and Future Projected Education Infrastructure for Raichur City[73]

Primary Education	UDPFI Guidelines (Population, Nos.)	Existing Infrastructure in Raichur City	Infrastructure Required for Raichur City	
			2011[a]	2021[b]
Pre-primary	1 for 2,500	11	21	36
Primary school (Class I-V)	1 for 2,500	17	21	36
Senior Sec. School (VI-XII)	1 for 7,500	7	7	12
Integrated School without Hostel (I-XII)	1 for 1,00,000	0	1	1
Integrated School with Hostel (I-XII)	1 for 1,00,000	0	1	1
School for handicapped	1 for 45,000	0	1	2
Higher Education				
College	1 for 1,25,000	10	1	1
Technical Education Centre	1 for 90,000	3	–	–
Polytechnic	1 for 90,000	3	–	–
Industrial Training Institute	1 for 90,000	2	–	–

a –By 2011, the population in the age-group of 5-14 yrs., and 15 to 24 yrs., has been calculated as 53,000 persons (20 % of the total population of 2,65,000).[73]

b –By 2021, the population by the age-group of 5-14 yrs., and 15 to 24 yrs., has been calculated as 90,000 persons (18 % of the total population of 5,00,000).[73]

Considering the poor child literacy rate, as discussed in Chapter 4, and the lack of enough pre-primary schools, it becomes imperative to focus on increasing the infrastructure for pre-primary schools.

As per the recommendations of Urban Development Plans Formulation and Implementation Guidelines[72], in the next couple of years Raichur would require another 10 pre-primary schools, one integrated school without hostel facility and one with hostel facility, and a special school for handicapped.

Health

The medical infrastructure of Raichur city have been surveyed, mapped and presented as Figure 5.3.

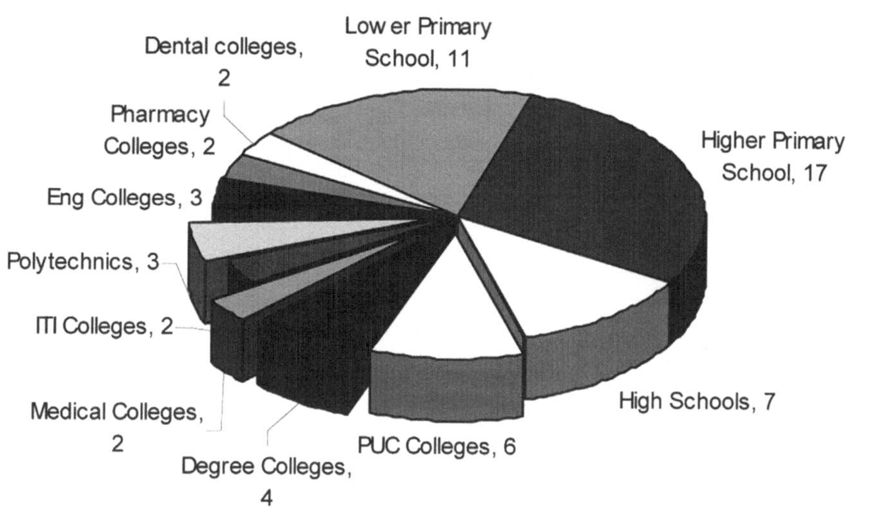

Fig. 5.2: Present Status of the Education Infrastructure of Raichur City

Presently Raichur has two government hospitals – one general hospital and two super specialty hospital (Rajiv Gandhi Super Specialty Hospital, run by Oil Producing and Exporting Countries), one Ayurvedic (Unani) hospital, 15 nursing homes, and 4 polyclinics (Figure 5.4 and Table 5.2). Apart from these, Navodaya Medical College Hospital and Research Centre with 1000 beds is operated by a private institute and a new medical college and hospital – Raichur Institute of Medical Sciences with facility for 1000 beds is under construction. This medical infrastructure for a population of 2,65,000 (projected population for 2011) is not adequate.

From Table 5.2 it can be inferred that Raichur needs another three intermediate hospitals. Though there are 15 nursing homes with facilities for child welfare and maternity care and 20 dispensaries which is at par with the desired bench mark of Urban Development Plans Formulation and Implementation Guidelines, they are not strategically located geographically (Figure 5.3). It is recommended that any new medical facilities that are likely to come up, and even possibly relocate the existing ones, such that all the residents of the city can have access to them with least effort.

Socio-cultural Facilities

Socio-cultural facilities such as: recreation centres, cinema theatres, gardens and playgrounds, grave yards and police stations have been presented as Figure 5.5.

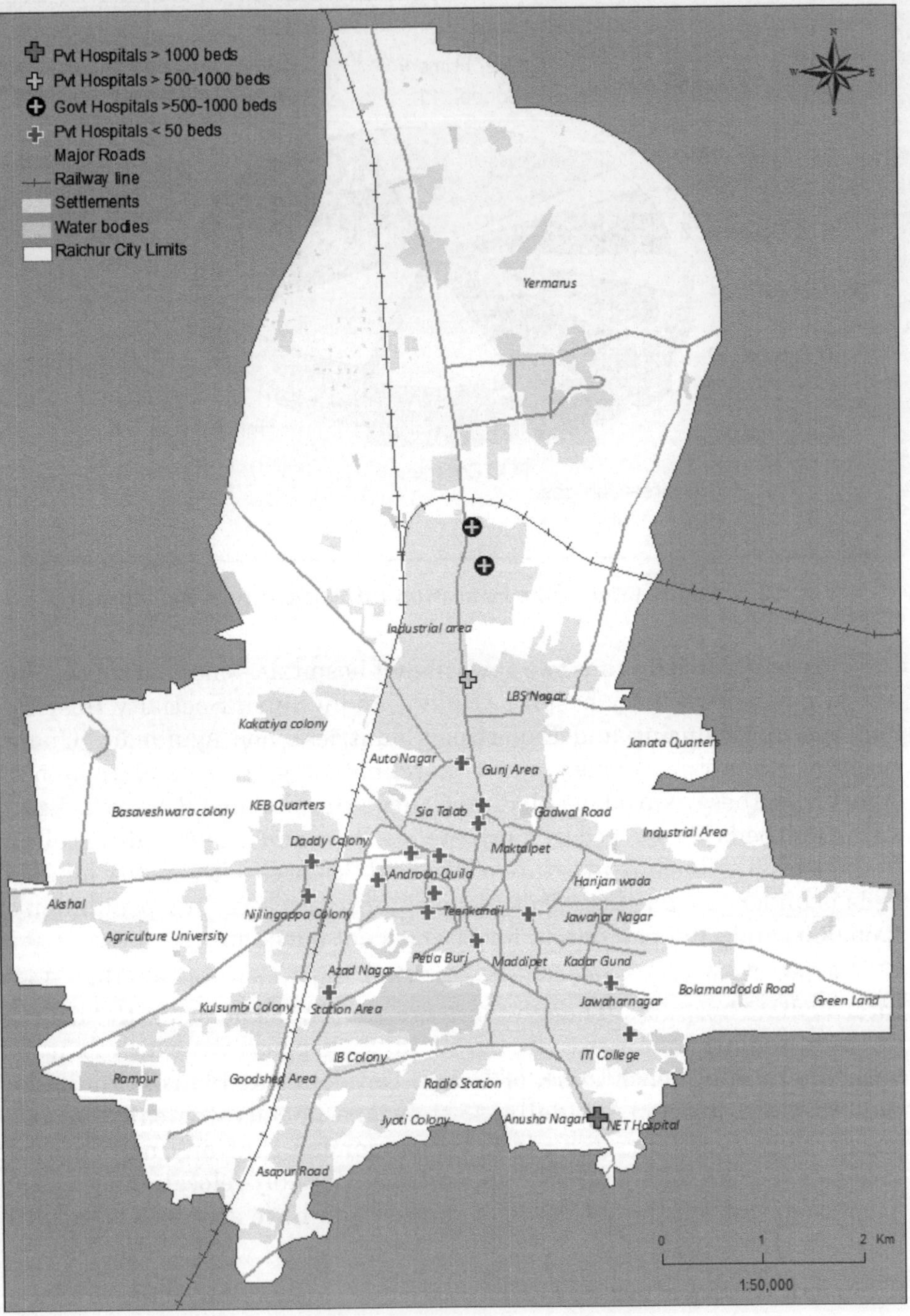

Fig. 5.3: Distribution of Hospitals Across Raichur City

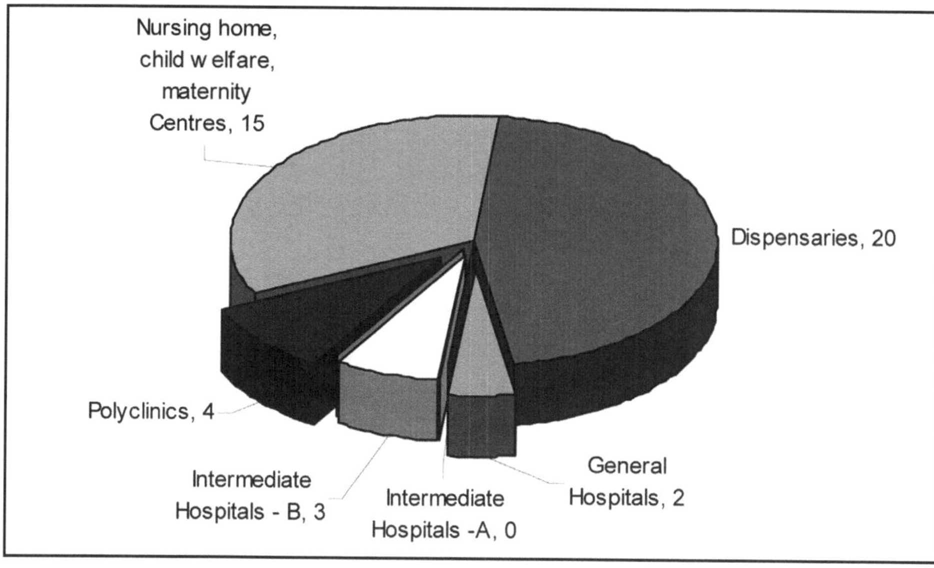

Fig. 5.4: Present Status of the Health Infrastructure of Raichur City

Table 5.2: The Existing and Future Projected Health Infrastructure for Raichur City[73]

Health	UDPFI Guidelines	Facilities	Existing Infrastructure in Raichur City	Facilities	Infrastructure Required for Raichur City	
					2011[a]	2021[b]
General Hospital	1 for 250000 population	500 beds	2	250	1	2
Intermediate Hospital - A	1 for 100000 population	100 beds	0	–	3	5
Intermediate Hospital - B	1 for 1000000 population	50 beds, 10 maternity beds	3	–	0	1
Polyclinic	1 for 1000000 population	few observation beds	4	–	0	1
Nursing home, child welfare, maternity Centre	1 for 45000 population	–	15	–	6	11
Dispensary	1 for 15000 population	–	20	–	18	33

a – Considering the projected population of 2,65,000 population by 2011.[73]
b – Considering the projected population of 5,00,000 population by 2021.[73]

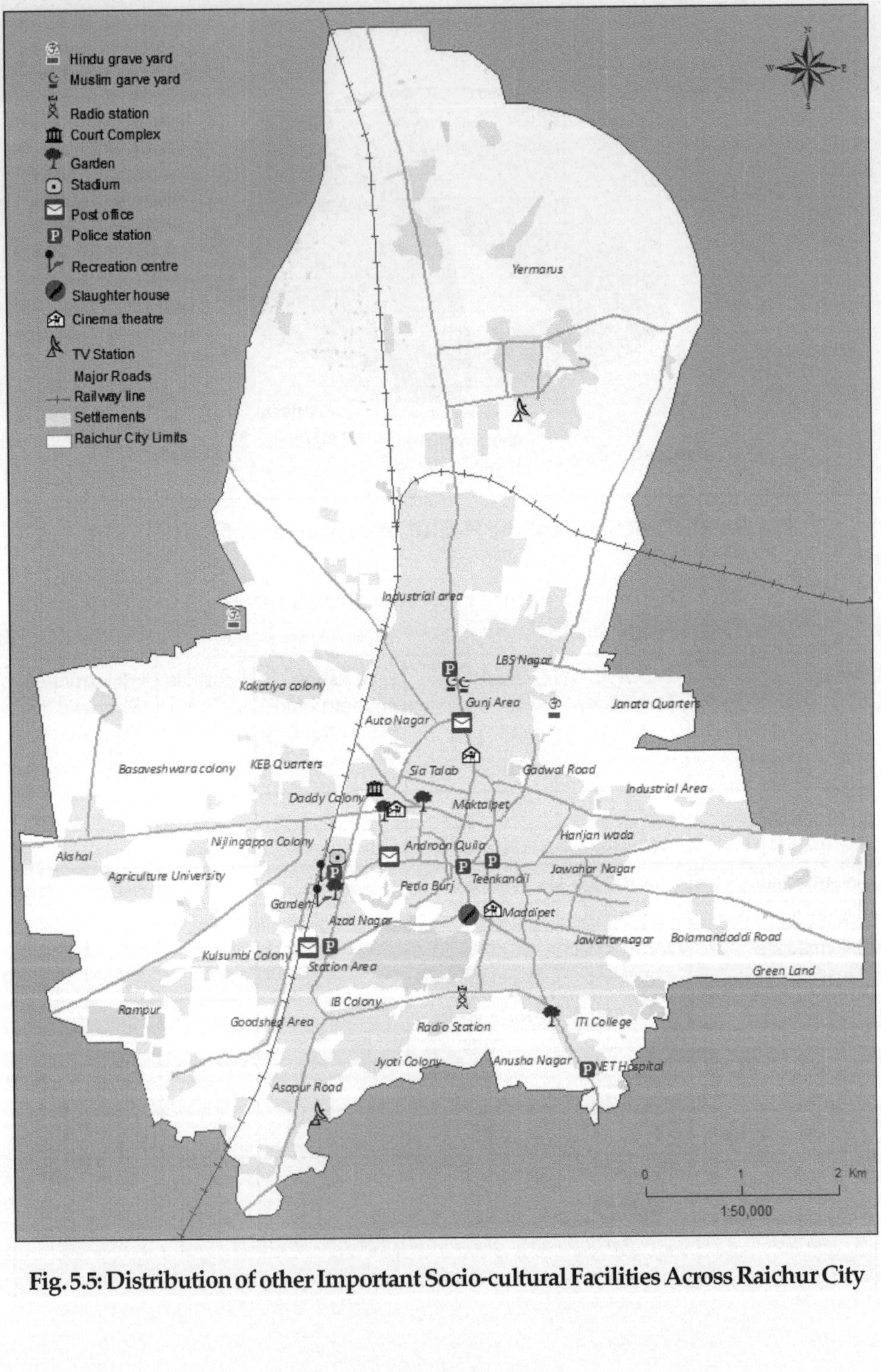

Fig. 5.5: Distribution of other Important Socio-cultural Facilities Across Raichur City

Raichur city lacks adequate parks and playgrounds as can be seen from the Raichur city map (Figure 5.5). The schools and colleges do not have adequate play grounds. Hence, it's very important to identify the areas that can be converted as parks and playgrounds within the city as well as in the outskirts of the city.

The city also needs 12 community halls, 53 community rooms, one more recreation club, and one more socio-cultural centre based on the population projections by 2011 and 2021 has been presented in Table 5.3.

There are two Hindu grave yards, one in the core of the city and the other one in the outskirts. Though there are two prominent Muslim graveyards at Gunj Road, most of the places even Dargas also are used as burial grounds.

Table 5.3: The Existing and Future Projected Socio-cultural Facilities for Raichur City[73]

Socio-cultural Facilities	UDPFI Guidelines	Existing Infrastructure in Raichur City	Facilities Required for Raichur by	
			2011[a]	2021[b]
Community room	1 for 5000 population	–	53	100
Community Hall and Library	1 for 15000 population	6	18	33
Recreation club	1 for 100000 population	2	3	5
Music, Dance and Drama Centre	1 for 100000 population	3	3	5
Meditation and Spiritual Centre	1 for 100000 population	2	3	5
Socio-cultural Centre	1 for 1000000 population	1	0	1

a – Considering the projected population of 2,65,000 population by 2011.[73]
b – Considering the projected population of 5,00,000 population by 2021.[73]

Law and order situation is maintained by five police stations and one district sessions court. The police stations are located as a cluster within one sq km., (Figure 5.5). It's pertinent that some of the police stations are relocated such that they are within the reach of civilians outside the core of Raichur city.

Religion

Raichur city has 52 temples, 27 Dargas, and 3 churches. The spatial distribution of the same has been presented as Figure 5.6. The thematic map demonstrates the religious bonhomie among the various communities – Hindus, Muslims and Christianity.

Most of the temples in Raichur are ancient and the spread of settlements correlate well with the location of temples.

ECONOMIC INFRASTRUCTURE

Agriculture Scenario

Vast stretches of land, towards west of Raichur city, come under the irrigation facilities of Tungabhadra command area. In these areas, agriculturists are raising irrigated cotton, paddy and summer crops. Towards east of the city, one can find mostly rock outcrops and a few plantations that are irrigated by natural streams and surface water bodies.

The Raichur market for the agricultural produce - food grains, oil seeds and cotton was regulated in February 1934 under the Hyderabad Agricultural Market Act of 1939. In all 113 agricultural commodities are under regulation. As Raichur market is situated along the Mumbai-Chennai railway line and having other transport facilities, the prices in this market remain always attractive than the nearby markets. Hence, farmers and agricultural dealers of different Taluks bring their goods for sale here.

- *Markets:* The market area comprises the whole of Raichur Taluk and Deodurg Taluk. The market has a well built market yard known as Rajendra Gunj, comprising 29 ha. There are 120 shop-cum-godowns of uniform pattern and dimensions. These shops and godowns are owned by traders and commission agents. There are 410 traders and 216 commission agents. Every monday, a weekly shandy is held at Shandy Maidan, which is situated near Agricultural Produce Marketing Committee premises.

Market Sub Yards

- *Patel Road:* The whole sale business of food grains are carried at Patel road and it has been declared as sub-market.
- *New Cotton Market Yard*: On the Raichur-Hyderabad highway, a separate market for cotton transaction was established as sub-yard in the year 1995. It is 3 km., away from Main Market Yard.
- *Sub Market Yard*: The Market Committee has two sub-market yards *(i)* Deodurga Sub-Market, *(ii)* Jalahalli Sub-Market.

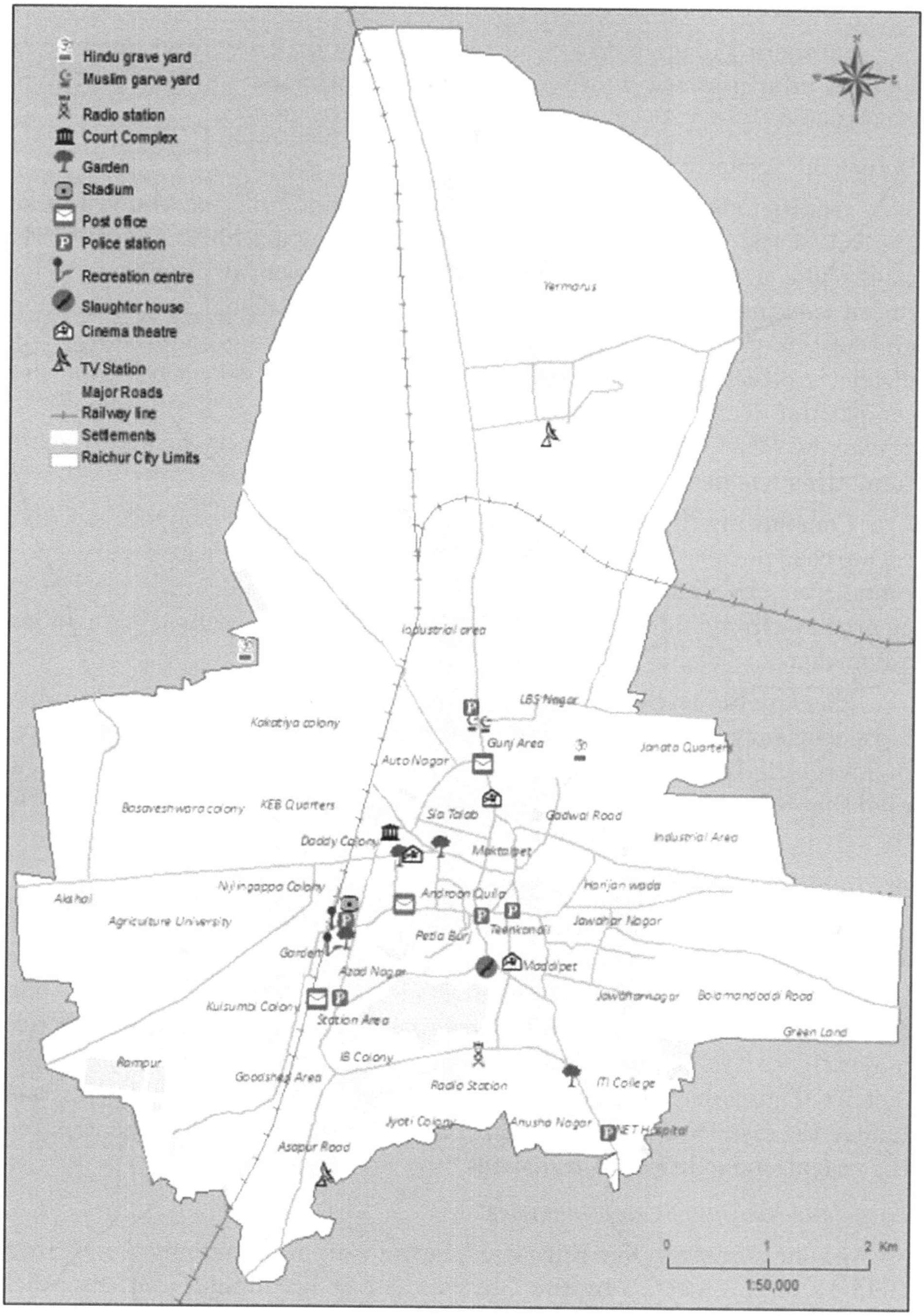

Fig. 5.6: Spatial Distribution of Religious Centres Across Raichur City

Rural Market

Yaragera Village is the rural market, 15 km., away from Raichur. It has an administrative office-cum-godown and an auction platform constructed.

Industrial Scenario

Traditionally Raichur District, along with Sindanur and Manvi Taluks are considered as rice bowls of Karnataka as they are blessed with world class paddy grown fields. Prior to 1990's, Raichur was also well known for the oil seeds and cotton industries. Due to lack of technological up gradation and cut-throat competition due to imports, it lost its base as one of the leading district in oil seed and cotton industries. In the last one decade due to severe competition from Multi-National Companies and large scale industries, driven by World Trade Organization, the growth rate of small scale Industries has been slowed down.

Considering the abundant natural resources such as: minerals, water resources, power, land availability, human resources; and very good connectivity by road and rail, there is a great potential in the district to emerge as strong industrial base. The proximity of Hyderabad is an added advantage.

The key industries and the supporting infrastructure of Raichur city have been surveyed, mapped and presented as Figure 5.7. From the figure, it can clearly be inferred that most of the rice mills are located along the road that leads to Gadwal, while a few other industries are located north of the city – in the industrial area and Yermarus.

Availability of Natural Resources

Raichur is well known for quality agriculture produce like: rice, sunflower, cotton, and horticultural produce like: mango, banana, and lemon. The main minerals in the district are gold, copper, iron, feldspar, granite, sandstone, quartz, and limestone. The district is blessed with two major rivers Krishna and Tungabhadra which provide water supply to the district. Tungabhadra Left Bank Canal irrigates about 80,000 hectares of land in the district. The Narayanpur Project on the River Krishna increased the irrigation facilities of the district.

Large and Medium Scale Industries

Major Industries like Karnataka Power Corporation Limited and Hutti Gold Mines are set up by the Government of Karnataka and the other medium scale industries are set-up by private firms (Table 5.4).

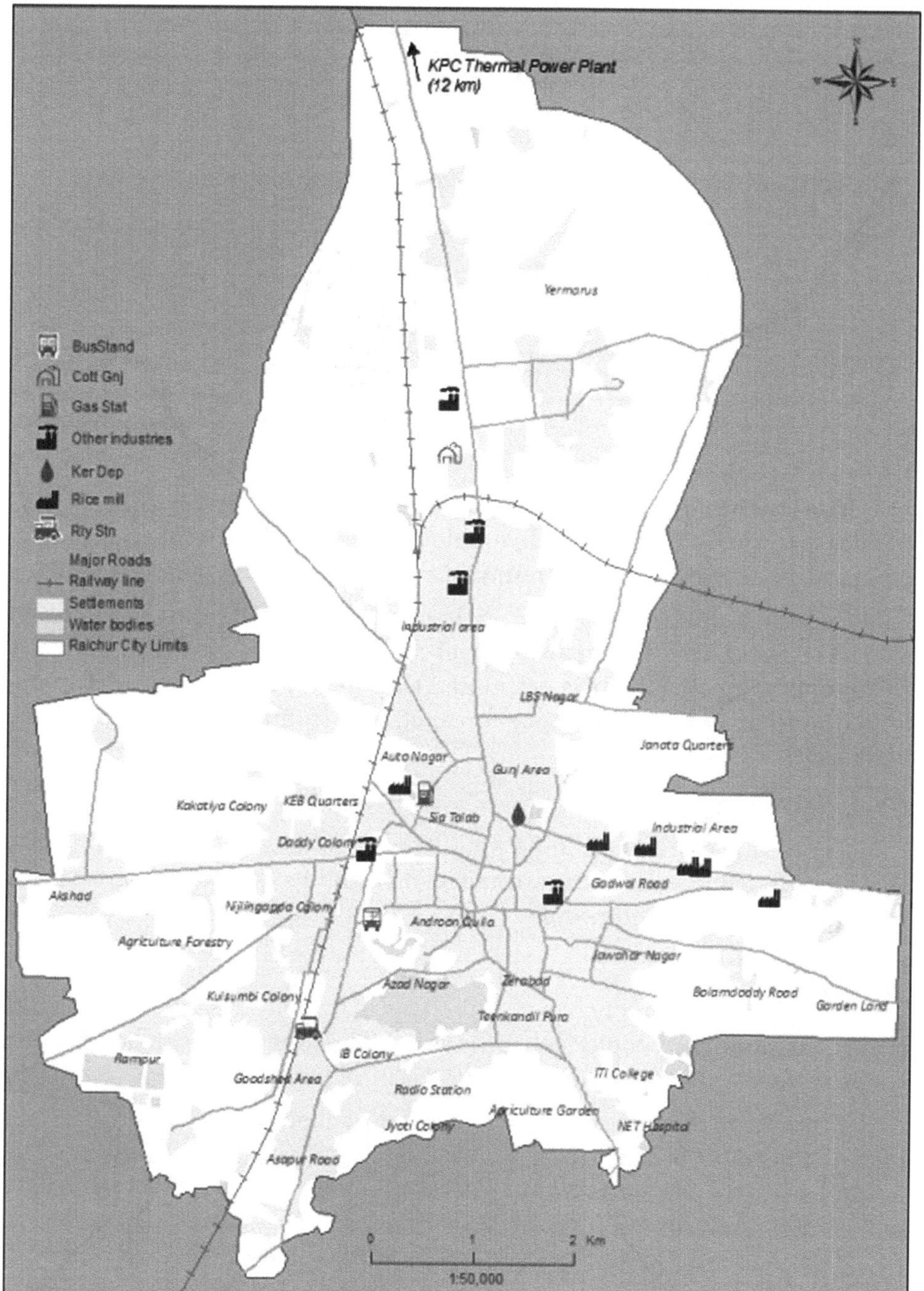

Fig. 5.7: Location of the key Industrial Establishments and the Supporting Infrastructure

Table 5.4 Major Industries Located in Raichur City[52]

Sl. No.	Name and Address of the Unit	Product	Employment
1.	M/s Hutti Gold Mine Company, Hutti, Lingsugur Taluk, Raichur (Dt).	Gold Mine	4018
2.	M/s Karnataka Power Corporation Ltd., Shakthinagar, Raichur (Dt)	Power Generation	2412
3.	Raichur Solvent, Raichur	Solvent Extraction	68
4.	General Oil Seeds Grower Co-operative Society Ltd., Raichur	Oil Seeds	74
5.	Farooq Anwar Company Raichur	Oil Refining	99
6.	Mysore Petro Chemical Ltd., Post Box No. 34, Raichur	Petro Chemical products	156

The Raichur Thermal Power Station in Shakthinagar (Figure 5.7) has 8 units, producing 210 MW each, employing ISO 14001, an internationally accepted specification for environmental management systems (EMS).

Surana Industries (P) Ltd., Vishvesvaraya Steel Plant (P) Ltd., and Central Power Grid Station are some of the major industries that are likely to be coming up shortly. It is estimated that nearly 25,000 workers would be required as part of the labour force, official staff, and other subsidiary workers.

Small Scale Sector

There are more than 2894 small scale industries registered in the District of Raichur, with an investment of 6,405 lakhs, providing employment to over twelve thousand people.

POWER SUPPLY

The electricity supply in Raichur city is in deficit. The city faces regular power cuts and the people feel that though Raichur produces power from the KPC thermal power plant, the city itself remains in dark.

From Figure 5.8, it can be inferred that residential sector is the second largest consumer of electricity followed by industries and commerce. The power losses are pegged at 22 to 23 per cent and the breakdown rate is 0.02 per cent for the year 2005 till 2008.

WATER SUPPLY AND SANITATION

Water supply and sanitation are important basic needs affecting the quality of life and productive efficiency of the people. Provision of these

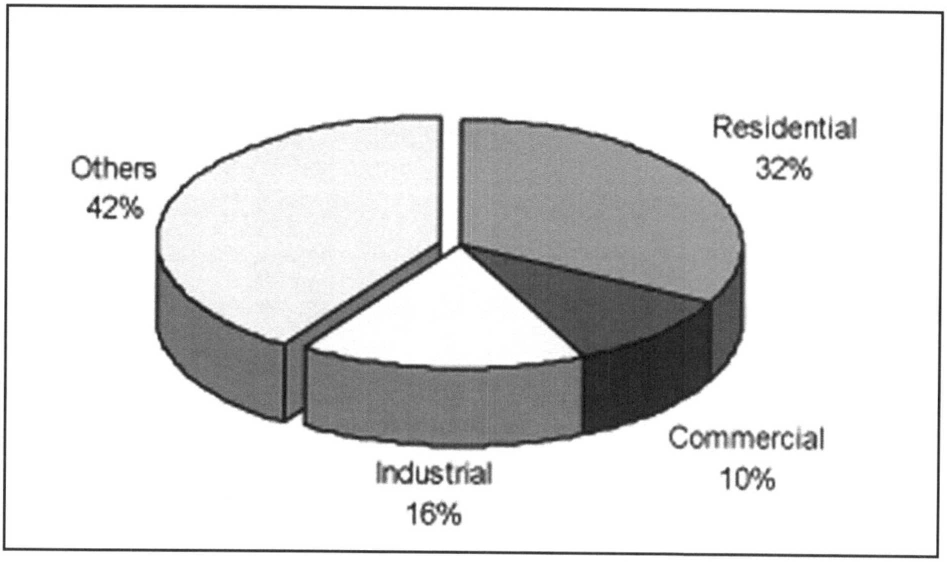

Fig. 5.8: The Typical Electricity Consumption Pattern for Raichur City

basic services continues to be among the core activities of urban local bodies. The State Governments and ULBs are responsible for providing the services through proper planning, implementation, operation and maintenance, and monitoring through the funds available under State Plans, internal resource generation and by taking loans from financial institutions.

Raichur city depends on both surface and ground water resources. Due to the proximity of Krishna and Tungabhadra rivers, the surface water is abundant. The main source of drinking water is River Krishna. From here, the water is pumped and treated at sump wells located at Rampura, Deosugur, and Chikka sugur (2nd Stage) villages. After treatment, the water is stored in 5 overhead tanks; from where the water is supplied to the entire city by gravitational flow. In addition to the surface water resources, there are 52 borewells spread across the city to augment the supply of drinking water.

The typical drinking water requirement for Raichur city being 24 million litres per day (MLD), currently 22.08 MLD is available for supply (Figure 5.9). The deficient of 1.92 MLD is not significant in the present day scenario. Nevertheless, considering the rapid urbanization and industrialization, the water supply infrastructure needs to be escalated without any delay.

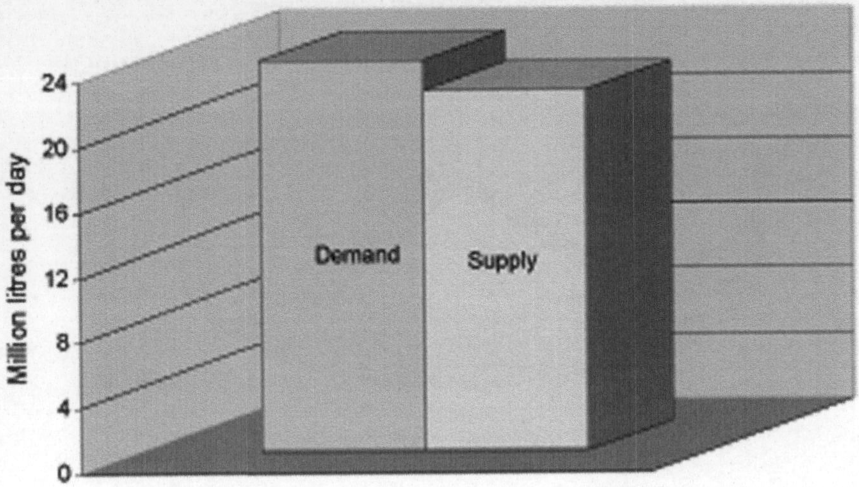

Fig. 5.9: The Drinking Water Demand and Supply for Raichur City

Under Ground Drainage (UGD)

The underground drainage is constructed and maintained by City Municipal Council of Raichur. Most of the residential areas are covered by UGD, covering an area of 1.69 sq km., with a running length of 80 km (Figure 5.10). Though the city had been growing over the years, the UGD network remained the same. It's imperative that the Raichur Municpal Authorities focus on improving the UGD to match with the growing population demand.

Solid Waste Management

According to the Municipal Solid Waste Management Rules 2000 enforced since Dec 1999, it is duty of every Municipal Body/ULB (Urban Local Body) to adopt suitable system of solid waste management. The city of Raichur generates 78 tonnes of solid waste per day. Of this, 50 tonnes of municipal solid waste is collected and disposed. The solid waste disposal site at Eklaspur village, spanning an area of 9 ha, is located in the outskirts of the city.

The integrated solid waste management project for Raichur city, sponsored by Indo-Norwegian Environment Programme and Directorate of Municipal administration, has come as breather for the citizens. Under this programme, CMC Raichur in partnership with Application of Science and Technology to Rural Areas (IISc, Bangalore) and Environment Support Group, has taken up the following tasks:

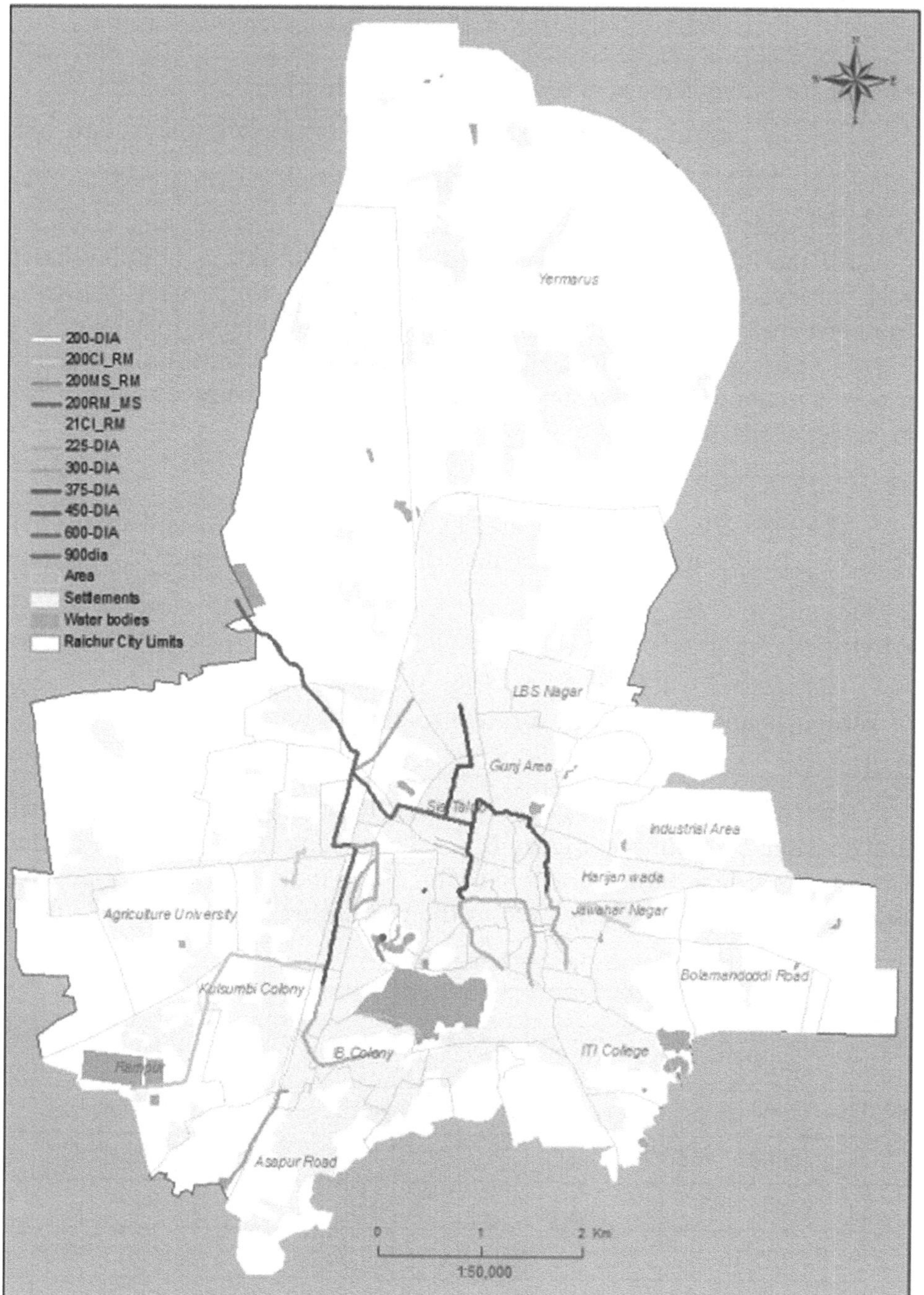

Fig. 5.10: The Existing Underground Drainage Network

- Promote segregation of waste at source.
- Conduct local awareness programme.
- Ensure involvement of public/NGO participation.
- Process organic waste by composting, vermi-composting and bio-methanation..

ADMINISTRATIVE BUILDINGS

All the administrative structures, both public and semi-public have been surveyed and mapped (Figure 5.11). Most of these offices are operating from private buildings with inadequate floor space and parking space, and narrow approach roads. Hence, it has been proposed to shift these offices to a new common, integrated building that is likely to come up within the premises of District office.

TRANSPORTATION

The city of Raichur is connected by roadways, railways and an airstrip (Figure 5.12). There are no ports, no coastline and no navigable rivers and canals.

Airstrip

The airstrip is located 4 km., from the heart of the city in the villages of Yermarus and Egnoor. The airstrip spans 248 ha.

Railways

Two broad gauge lanes pass through Raichur city connecting north and south of the country (Figure 5.12). These lanes link major cities like: Chennai, Mumbai, Bangalore, and Delhi. There is one Railway station with 3 platforms and one railway yard in the city (Table 5.5).

Table 5.5: Railway Details (as on April 2008)

Items	No's
No. of railway Stations	1
Types of rail gauge: broad, narrow and meter gauge	Broad gauge
Length of rail network (km.,)	6.5
No. of platforms	3
No. of yards	1

Data Source: SW Railway.

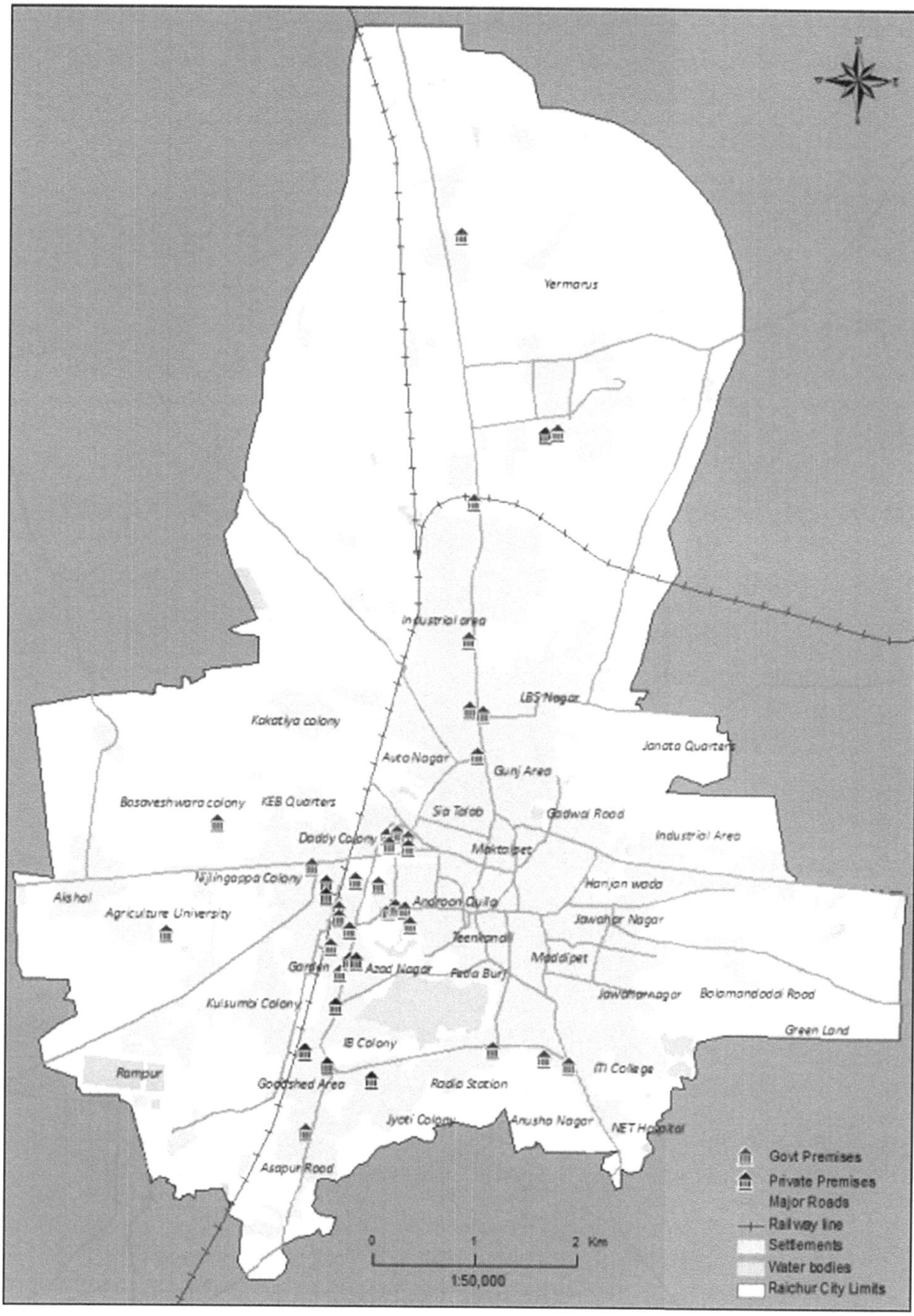

Fig. 5.11: Location of key Administrative Buildings of Raichur Categorized based on the Premises they are Operating from

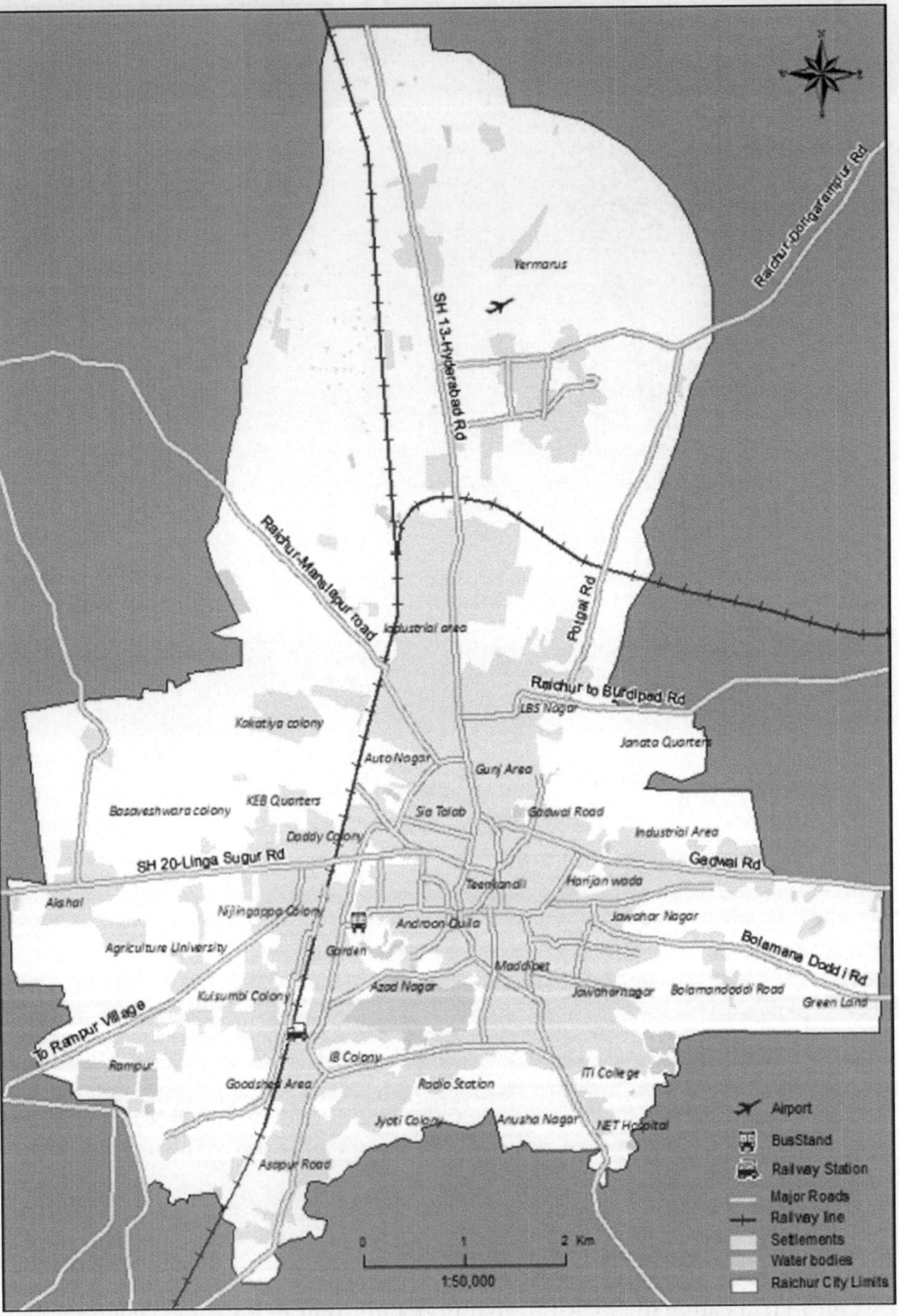

Fig. 5.12: Transportation Facilities in Raichur City

Roadways

Total running length of the roads in Raichur city is 476 km., (Table 5.6). Of this, 63 per cent (309 km.,) remain un-surfaced, *kuccha* roads, 34 per cent (166 km.,) are surfaced. There are no exclusive cycle tracks, and the footpaths span only 3 per cent (15.5 km.,) (Figure 5.13).

Table 5.6: Road Length and Footpath (Status as on March-April 2008)

Surfaced Road (km.)			Unsurfaced Road Length (km.)	Total Road Length (km.)	Foot Paths (km.)	Cycle Tracks (km.)
WBM	ASPHALT	CC				
79.1	70.13	17.60	309.17	476	15.5	NIL

Data Source: CMC, Raichur.

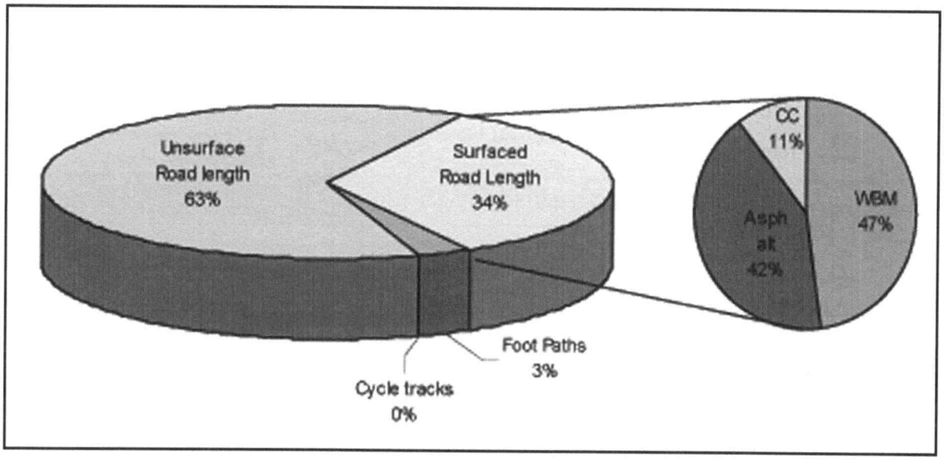

Fig. 5.13: Roads of Raichur city by Type and Surface

The water bound macadam (WBM) roads that were popular in the earlier days span 79 km., (47%) and the asphalt roads, the now popular among urban areas, cover about 70 km., (42%). The cement concrete (CC) roads span about 18 km., (11%) of the total surfaced roads (Figure 5.13).

The roadways need to be strengthened on war-foot basis considering that it's the back bone of any city.

TRAFFIC

A profile of the vehicles plying on the roads of Raichur indicate that maximum of them are light vehicles (72%) followed by non-motorized (26%) and heavy vehicles (2%) (Table 5.7 and Figure 5.14).

Among the light vehicles, 91 per cent are motorcycles and rest of them are cars, jeeps, auto rickshaws, omni buses, taxis and cabs. The non-motorized vehicles include cycles (89%), rickshaw, tonga, and others. Heavy vehicles comprise of trucks (56%) and buses (44%).

The total number of vehicles plying on the roads during 2005 till 2007 has increased by an average of 6 per cent. However, during 2007-08, there was a 25 per cent rise in the vehicles that has been contributed by the increase of motorcycles (30%) and auto rickshaws (25%) (Figure 5.15).

Considering that the maximum numbers of two wheelers are plying on the roads, a dedicated lane for them would help reduce the traffic congestion and decrease the time spent by them on roads.

Traffic Flow

The important roads that connect Raichur to the nearby places are:

1. State Highway No. 13, which connects Hyderabad and Mantralayam via Raichur.
2. State Highway No 20, which connects Raichur and Belgaum via Lingasugur.

Table 5.7: Registered Vehicles (2007)

Type of Vehicles		No. of Vehicles
Heavy vehicles	Trucks	
	Public	55
	Private	687
	Buses	
	Public	549
	Private	33
Light vehicles	Two wheelers	50,239
	Car	1,240
	Jeep	1,138
	Three wheelers	1,200
	Omni Buses	840
	Taxies/Cabs	314
Non-motorized (Unregistered)	Cycle	18,000
	Rickshaw	1,517
	Tonga	186
	Others	455

Data Source: District RTO Office.

The other internal major roads that enable the flow of traffic in Raichur are:

1. Station road.
2. Gunj road.
3. Jail road.
4. Patel road.
5. Nethaji road.
6. Basaveshwara road.
7. M G Road.

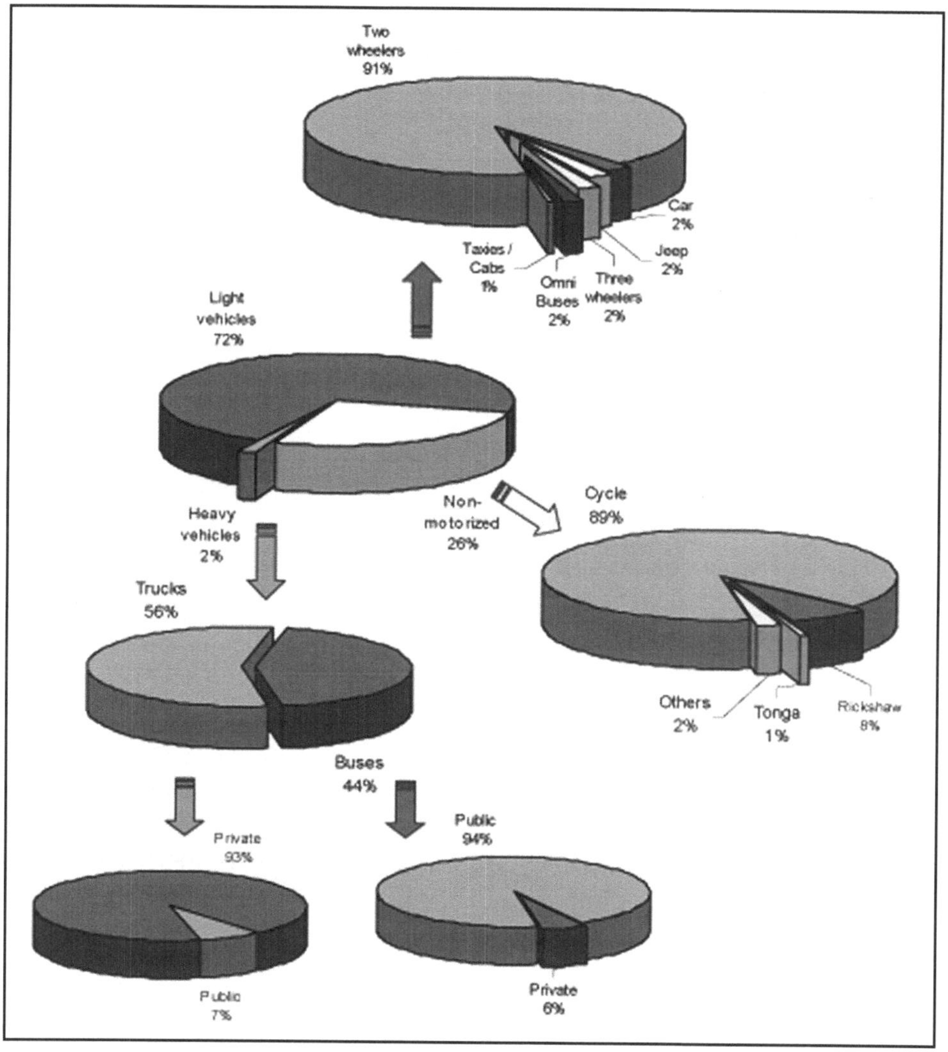

Fig. 5.14: Profile of the Vehicular Traffic of Raichur City

(Source: District RTO Office)

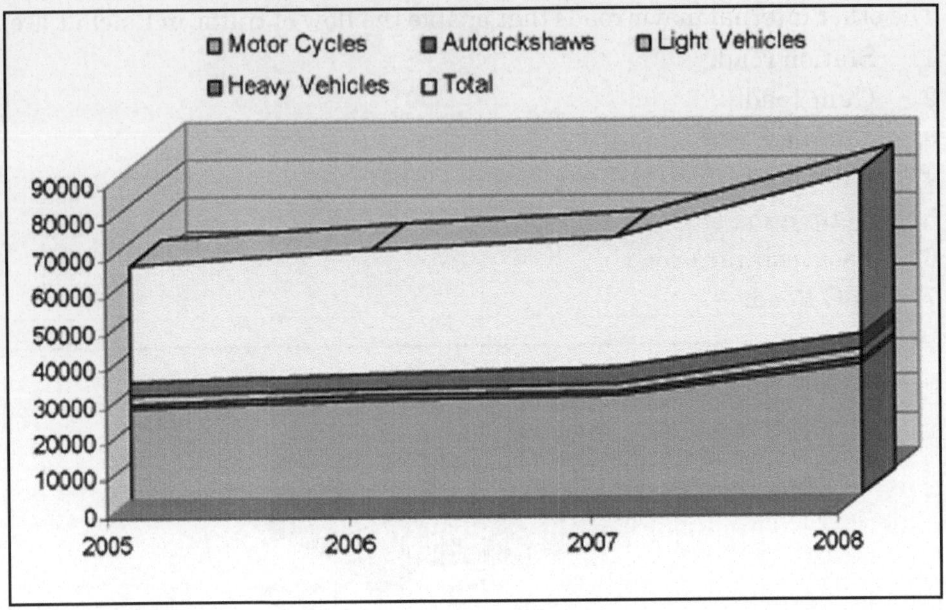

Fig. 5.15: The Increase in the Number of Vehicles Across the Years 2005 till 2008

(Source: District RTO Office)

State Highway (SH)

State Highways have a carriage width of 5.5 meters and formation width of 7.5 meters. The remaining roads were below 7.5 meters of formation width (bituminous black top) (Figure 5.16).

The passenger count units (PCU) and the total number of vehicles plying along the road were highest in the case of SH 20 (Lingasugur road) compared to the other roads.

Among the different types of vehicles, commercial vehicles were highest followed by the two-wheelers on all the roads.

The composition of slow moving vehicles was very less compared to the fast moving vehicles. Nevertheless, the slow moving vehicles can significantly disrupt the flow of traffic.

The vehicle damage factor (VDF) was the highest (5) for SH 20 followed by other roads. Thus it is important that SH 20 be widened the earliest in view of the traffic volume and the VDF.

Internal Roads

A majority of the traffic originating in the city passes through station road that connects railway station and bazaar area. Also most of the traffic passes through central business district.

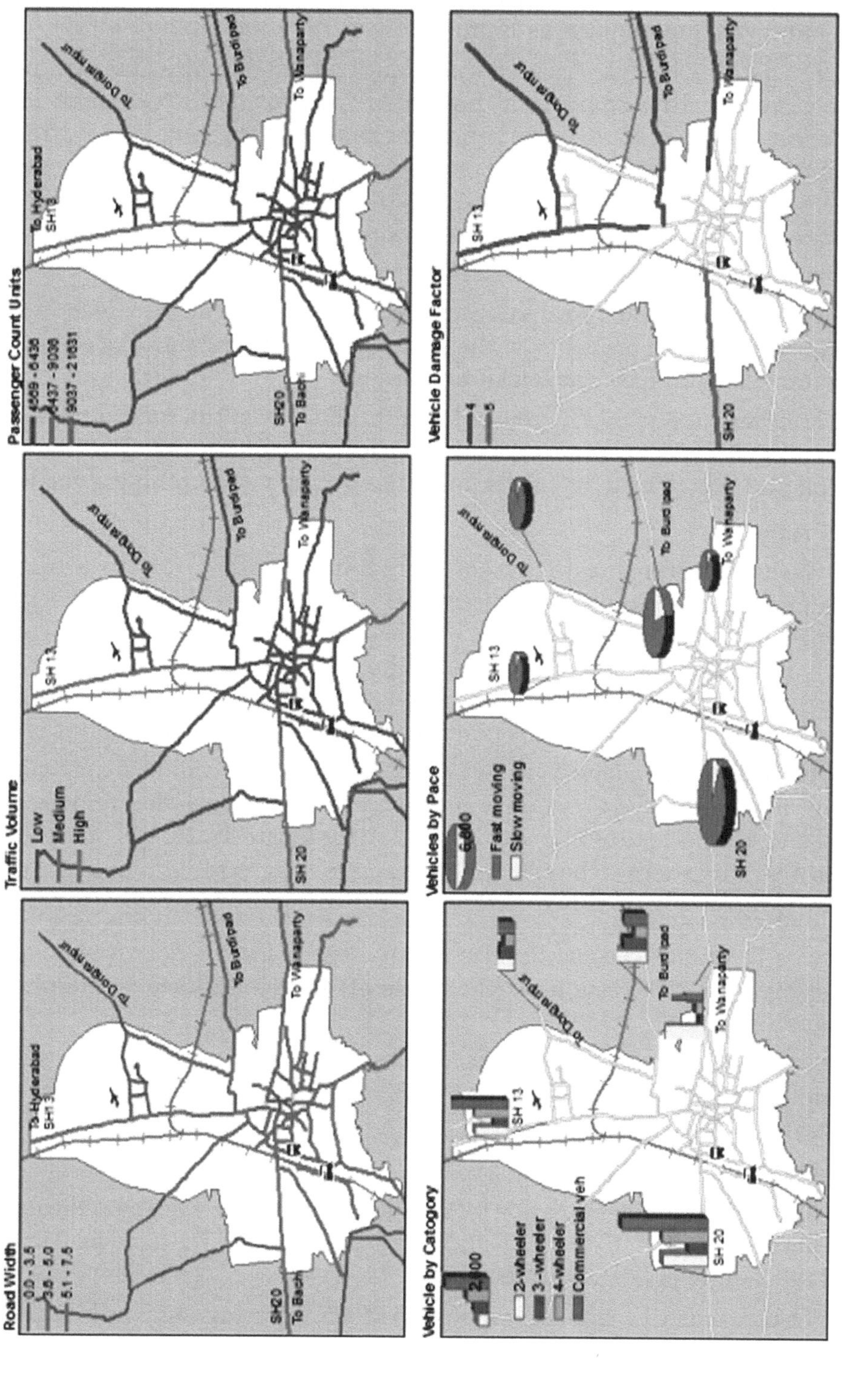

Fig. 5.16: Traffic Analysis for Major Roads, 2008

The important roads with heavy traffic flow and the junctions have been surveyed and mapped as Figure 5.17.

The pattern, insufficient road width, and bad intersections at important places cause traffic snarls and hazards. The crowded areas such as: Mahaveer chowk, vegetable market, teen khandeel circle have very narrow roads with poor road surface.

These roads need to be widened and resurfaced for easy and quick traffic flow. As the pedestrian traffic is also more in these areas, special provision must be made for pedestrians.

Widening of roads, formation of proposed roads and run roads will help mitigate traffic problems of the city. Well designed traffic circles need to be provided at important road junctions.

Road side trees help increase the aesthetic look of the roads and also they bring down the pollution levels and local temperatures. Thus, road side plantations need to be taken up on the existing and upcoming roads.

Mass Transit

Karnataka State Road Transport Corporation (KSRTC) is the sole mass transit provider in the city. The buses run by KSRTC provide access to some areas and the frequency is considerably less due to shortage of buses. This clearly indicates the steep rise in motorcycles and auto rickshaws, where the people have to depend on alternate ways of commuting. This mode of transit is harmful for the environment as it increases vehicular pollution.

The well designed mass transit indicates a successful and efficient city. Hence, it's imperative to improve present transit system. The number of buses and trips need to be increased such that the whole city can get adequate access travelling across the city.

Terminals

Bus Terminal. The bus stand of Raichur city is located near Ambedkar circle (Figure 5.12). From here, the buses ply between Raichur and other villages and cities.

Truck Terminal. As there is no truck terminal, Raichur District Administration has proposed to form the truck terminal with an extent of 10 acres.

Parking

Except from Railway station to Ambedkar Circle, there are no dedicated parking lots. Bus stand, Gunj Road, Market area, and teen Khandeel Circle need immediate provision for parking.

The authorities need to ensure that the existing shopping malls, restaurants and cinema halls to have adequate parking space. It should be

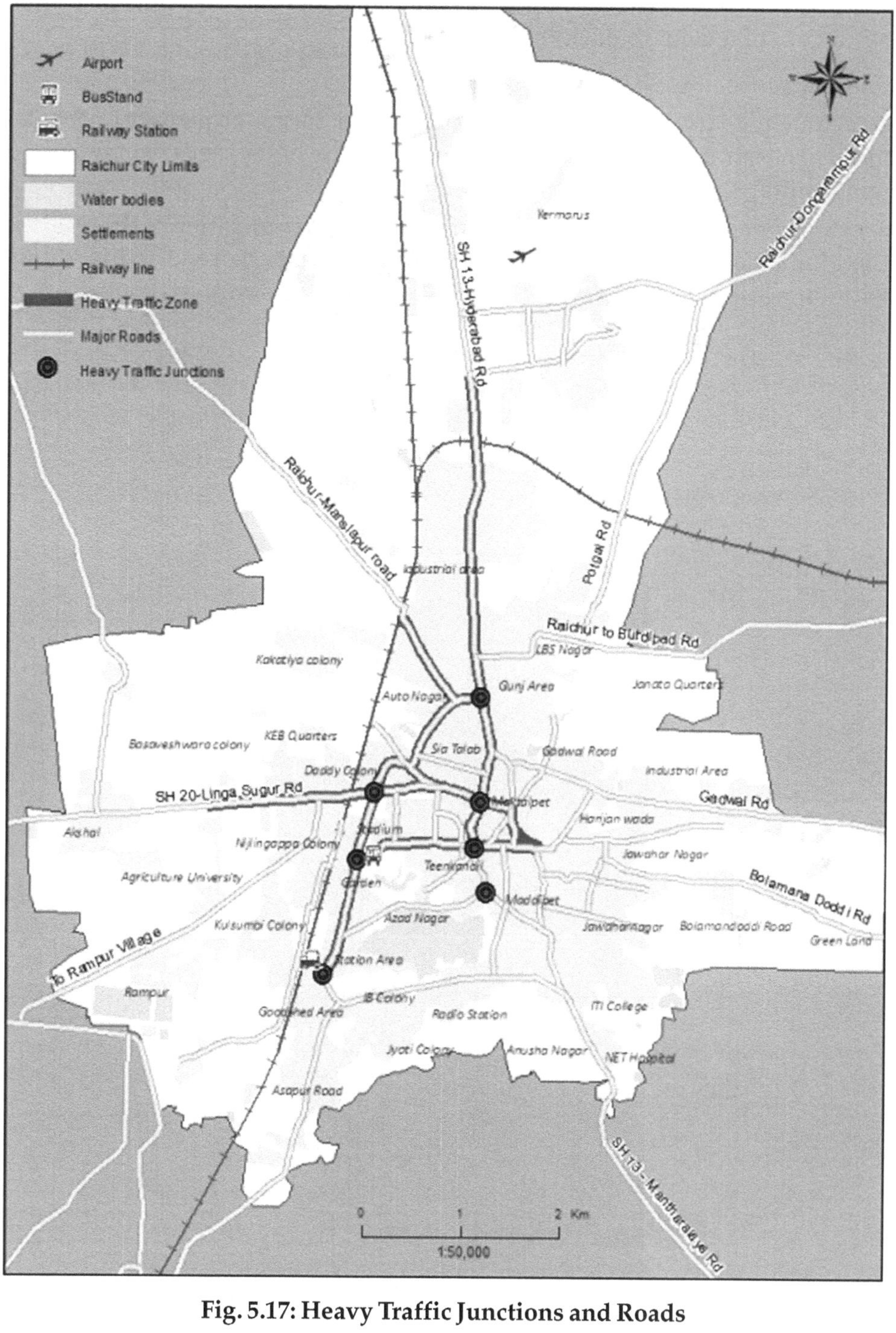

Fig. 5.17: Heavy Traffic Junctions and Roads

ensured that all the new buildings be sanctioned for construction only after assurance of adequate parking facilities.

Summary

Raichur city lacks adequate facilities in terms of primary schools, medical hospitals, parks, playgrounds, community halls, roads, water supply and drainage infrastructure.

Considering the rapid urbanization and industrialization of this region, the Municipal authorities should focus on providing the required facilities with immediate focus on water supply and drainage infrastructure.

6

URBAN SPRAWL OF RAICHUR CITY

METRICS AND DYNAMICS

INTRODUCTION

Urban sprawl refers broadly to the excessive growth of urbanization.[74] Often, rapid population growth and large scale migration leads to the phenomenon of urban sprawl. Some of the heavy criticisms of this phenomenon include depletion of natural resources, lack of basic amenities and low quality of life. The rapid shift of the world from rural to urban has made it imperative for further research in understanding the dynamics of urban sprawl which would help in evolving appropriate management strategies for sustainable development, effective resource utilization and provision of basic civic amenities.

Urban sprawl can be quantified using the various concepts and methods adopted from landscape metrics. Landscape metrics refer to the indices developed for describing categorical map patterns. Landscape metrics are algorithms that quantify specific spatial characteristics of patches, classes of patches, or entire landscape mosaics. These metrics can broadly be categorised as those that quantify the composition of the map without reference to spatial attributes, and those that quantify the spatial configuration of the map, requiring spatial information for their calculation.[79,80]

At landscape level, Geographic Information Systems (GIS), Remote Sensing and other software packages support quantification, monitoring, modeling and predicting urban sprawl. Landscape fragmentation information which when combined with the time series land cover information provides information on the type of change that is occurring in the landscape at a detailed scale. [17, 31, 34, 41, 75]

The ability to assess, measure, and monitor sprawl depends upon the availability of relevant, accurate, reliable data [37] and the appropriate mapping techniques. In a unique and relevant study, Epstein *et al.* [38] have assessed that for suburban areas with low density of houses GIS method results in better accuracy when compared to the unsupervised classification method using image processing techniques.

The authors Sudhira *et al.* [46] have quantified the sprawls of Mangalore-udipi highway by metrics of Shannon's entropy, patchiness and map density. To better understand the dynamics of sprawl it is imperative to model and predict the future course of sprawl. [46, 77, 78]

The authors Li and Yeh [75] have demonstrated how enforcing land use policies can influence the direction and magnitude of landscape change over the years. They have accomplished measurement of spatial patterns over two time periods by using indicators of compactness index and entropy.

DATA COLLECTION AND METHODOLOGY

Survey of India (SOI), 1982 toposheet on 1:25,000 scale has been used as base map for land-use and land-cover delineation. The satellite imagery for Raichur city was procured for the years 1998, 2002, 2009 from NRSC (National Remote Sensing Centre), Hyderabad.

The demographic data for Raichur city was collected from various sources such as: Directorate of Census and Municipal Council of Raichur.

Satellite imagery and SOI toposheets were classified using ERDAS Imagine 9.0 and ArcGIS 9.1. For Landscape analysis Spatial Analyst (ArcGIS 9.2) and Fragstat [43] were used.

RESULTS AND DISCUSSION

Map Composition

Map composition refers to features associated with the variety and abundance of patch types within the landscape, but without considering the spatial character, placement, or location of patches within the mosaic. Because composition requires integration over all patch types, composition metrics are only applicable at the landscape-level. There are many quantitative measures of landscape composition, including the proportion of the landscape in each patch type, patch richness, patch evenness, and patch diversity. Indeed, because of the many ways in which diversity can be measured, there are literally hundreds of possible ways to quantify landscape composition. Unfortunately, because diversity indices are derived from the indices used to summarize species diversity in community ecology, they suffer the same interpretative drawbacks. The important measures of composition are proportional abundance, richness, evenness, and diversity.

Diversity is a composite measure of richness and evenness and can be computed in a variety of forms such as: Shannon's diversity index and Simpson diversity index.

Shannon's Entropy (H_n)

Shannon's diversity index is a popular measure of diversity in community ecology that has been applied to landscapes to measure the richness and evenness. Shannon's index, referred to as Shannon's entropy (H_n), is sensitive to rare patch types than Simpson's diversity index[79]. H_n increases as the number of different patch types increases and/or the proportional distribution of area among patch types becomes more equitable. The Shannon's entropy (H_n), is given by the following equation,

$$H_n = \Sigma P_i \log_e(P_i) \quad (1)$$

where P_i is the proportion of the spatial variable in the ith zone and n is the total number of zones. This value ranges from 0 to log n, indicating very compact distribution for values closer to 0. The values closer to log n indicates that the distribution is much dispersed. Larger value of entropy reveals the occurrence of urban sprawl.

Figure 6.1 and Table 6.1 shows the built-up area, population and Shannon's entropy for 1982, 1998, 2002 and 2009. The results indicate that the distribution of built-up area in the region in 1982 was less dispersed than other years. However, the degree of dispersion has come down marginally in the year 2002 and has increased in the year 2009. Shannon's entropy correlates well with the built-up area and the population.

Table 6.1: Entropy Values, Built-up area and Population Across the Years

Year	Shannon's Entropy (H_n)	Built-up Area (sq km.,)	Population
1982	0.8926	4.62	124762
1998	1.4128	12.52	–
2002	1.2755	12.99	207421
2009	1.4318	19.33	–

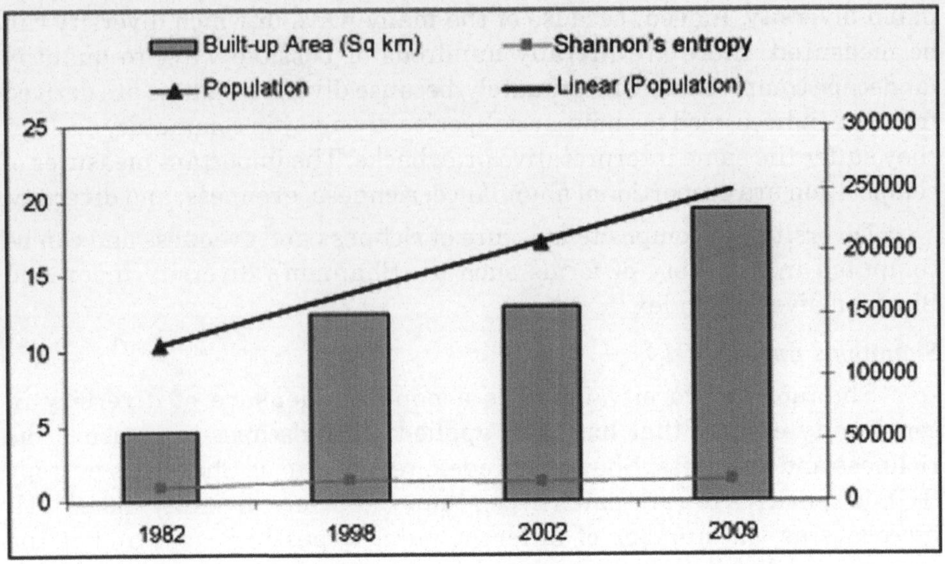

Fig. 6.1: Shannon's Entropy, Built-up area and population for Raichur City

Patchiness

Patchiness or the number of different classes (NDC) is the measurement of the density of patches of all types or number of clusters within the n×n window. In other words, it is a measure of the number of heterogeneous polygons over a particular area. Greater the patchiness more heterogeneous the landscape is. [81] In this case, the density of patches among different categories was computed for a 3×3 window. The computation of patchiness using 3×3 moving window revealed that five heterogeneous classes category was maximum (85.71%) and six heterogeneous classes category was the least (14.28%) in the study area (Table 6.2). This reveals that about 57.14 per cent of the study area is homogeneous while the rest are heterogeneous with patch classes ranging from two to five (Figure 6.2).

Table 6.2: Percentage Distribution of Patchiness

Number of Classes	Percentage Distribution
1.	57.14
2.	42.85
3.	71.42
4.	28.57
5.	85.71
6.	14.28

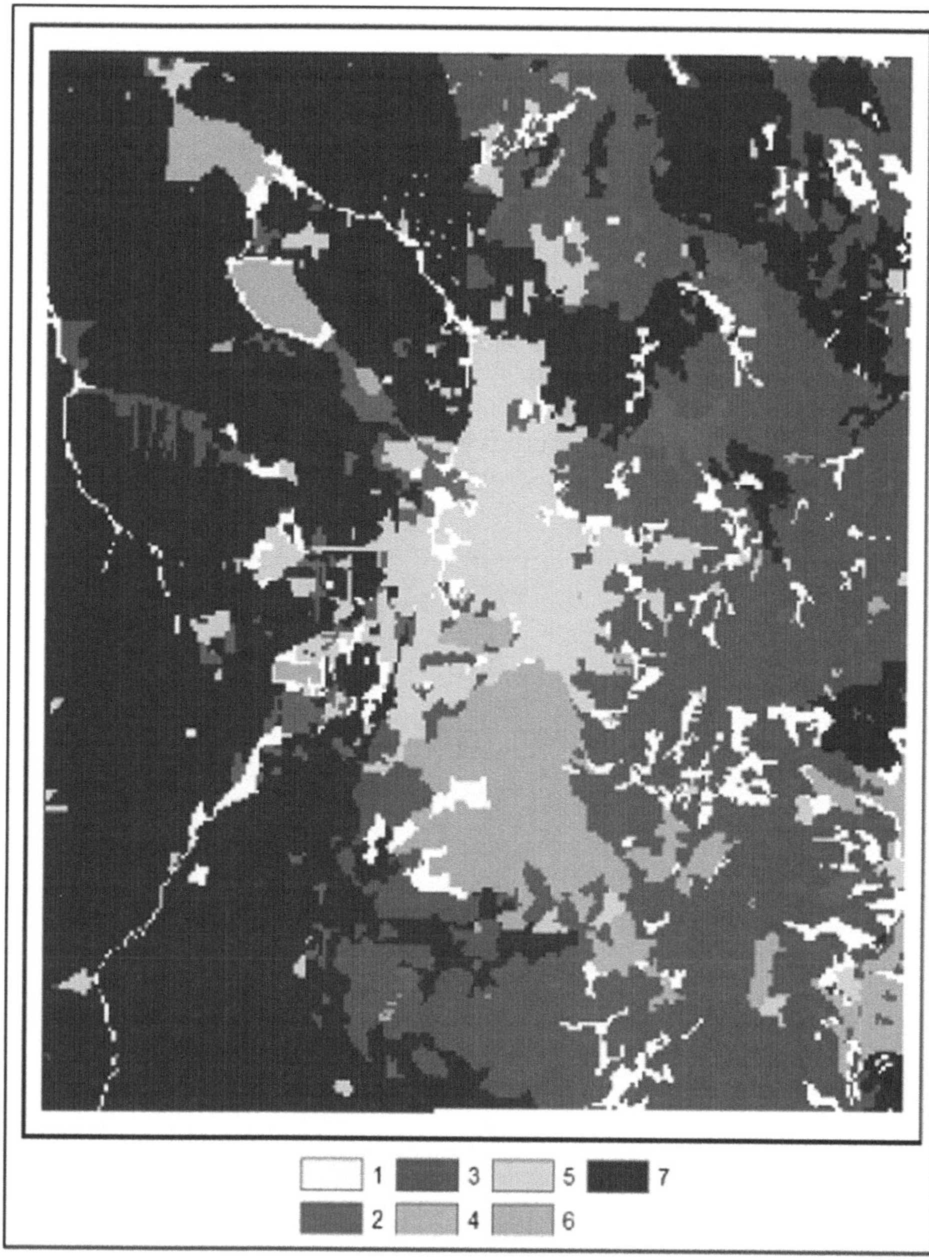

Fig. 6.2: GRID Showing the Patchiness or the Number of Different Classes (NDC)

Map Density

Map density values are computed by dividing number of built up pixels to the total number of pixels in a kernel. This when applied to a classified satellite image converts landcover classes to density classes, which is given in Figure 6.3. Depending on the density levels, it could be further grouped as low, medium and high density (Table 6.3). Based on this, relative share of each category was computed (area and percentage). This enabled in identifying different urban growth centres and sub-sequently correlating the results with Shannon's entropy for identifying the regions of high dispersion.

The computation of built-up density gave the distribution of the high, medium and low-density built-up clusters in the study area. High density of built-up would refer to clustered or more compact nature of the built-up theme, while medium density would refer to relatively lesser compact built-up and low density referred to loosely or sparsely spread built-up areas.

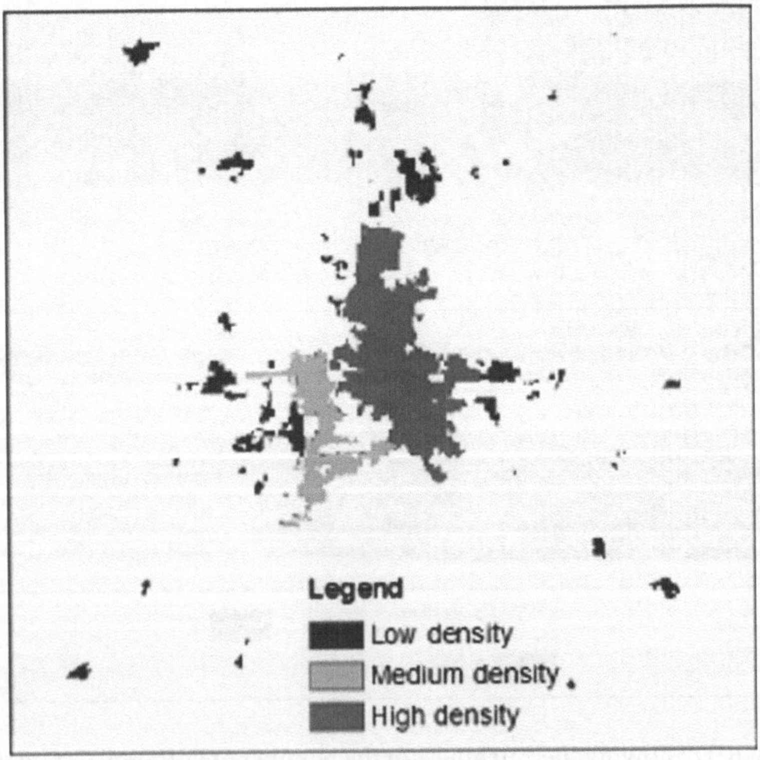

Fig. 6.3: Map Showing the Density of built-up Areas

Table 6.3: Density-based Classification of Built-up area for 2009

Category	Area (sq km.,)	Percentage
Low density	6.6	34.38
Medium density	3.2	16.67
High density	9.4	48.96

The percentage of low-density built-up area was only 34.38 per cent as against 16.67 per cent of medium density and as much as 48.96 per cent of high-density built-up area (Table 6.3). This reveals that more compact or highly dense built-up was the highest followed by more dispersed or least dense built-up. An important inference that could be drawn out of this was that high and low density built-up areas were found all along the highways along with the city centres. Most of the high density was found to be within and closer to the core of Raichur city. However, medium density was also found mostly along the city periphery. This further substantiates the results of Shannon's entropy, which revealed a high dispersion of the built-up theme in the study area.

Land-use Change Analysis

Land-use and land-cover change analysis gives an insight into the genesis and the underlying cause of urban sprawl. For Raichur city, a thorough land-use/land-cover change analysis was done to check which categories were converted to settlements (Table 6.4). The results indicate that between 1982 and 2009, a majority of miscellaneous land-use category (947 ha, 58%) has been converted to settlements (Figure 6.4). Nearly 23 per cent of agriculture lands, 14 per cent of scrub land, 3 per cent plantations, 1 per cent water bodies, and 0.26 per cent of forest land were developed as built-up areas. Thus in the last 27 years 1,625 ha of land was converted to settlements (Figure 6.5 and 6.6).

Except for Am Talab, most of the other small water bodies were encroached and converted to settlements. The south-east portion of forest area, near Mantralaya road, has been converted to agriculture garden. Interestingly, most of the land-use categories that were converted to settlements were within a reach of 500 m from roads.

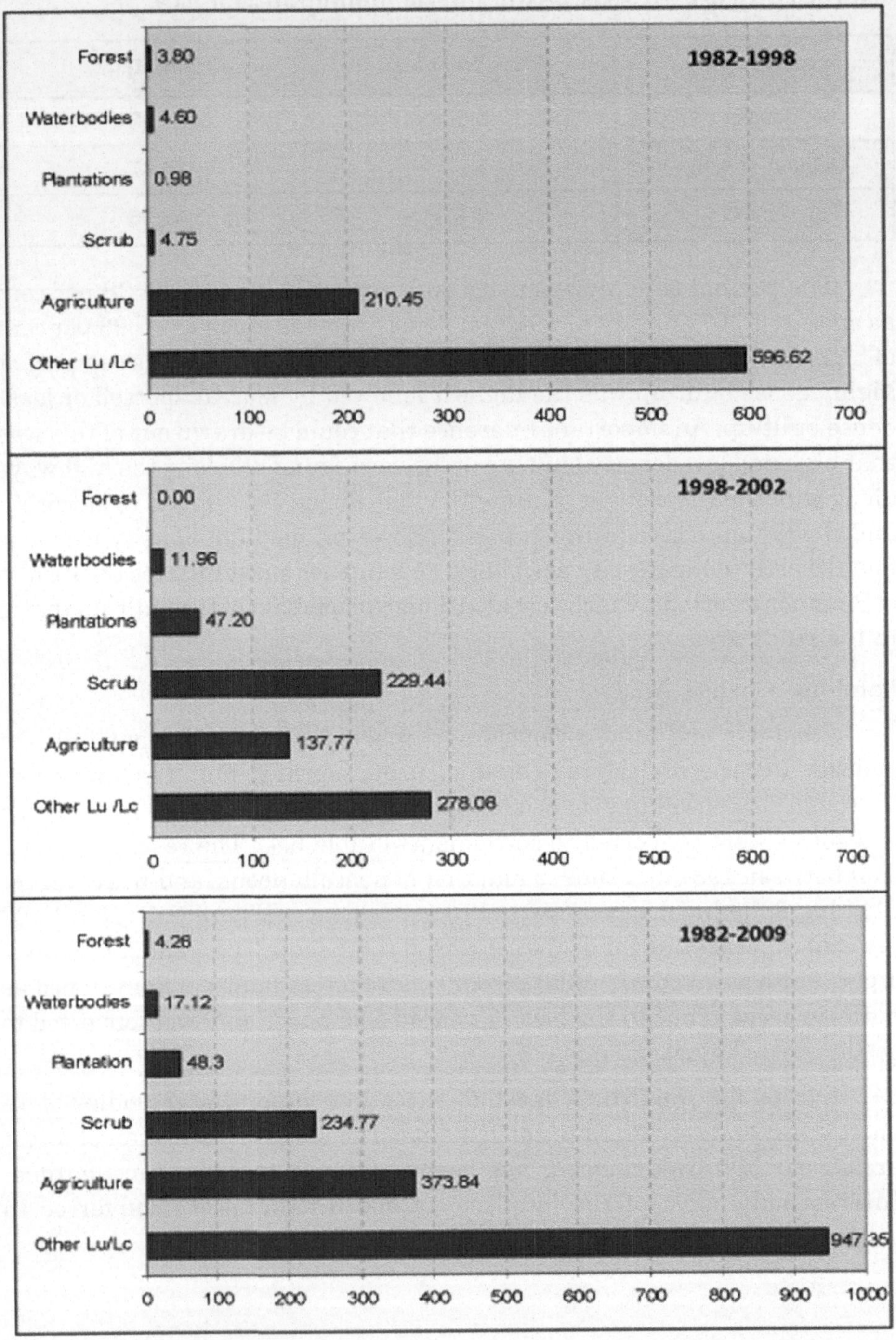

Fig. 6.4: Land-use, Land-cover Categories (ha) Converted to Settlements

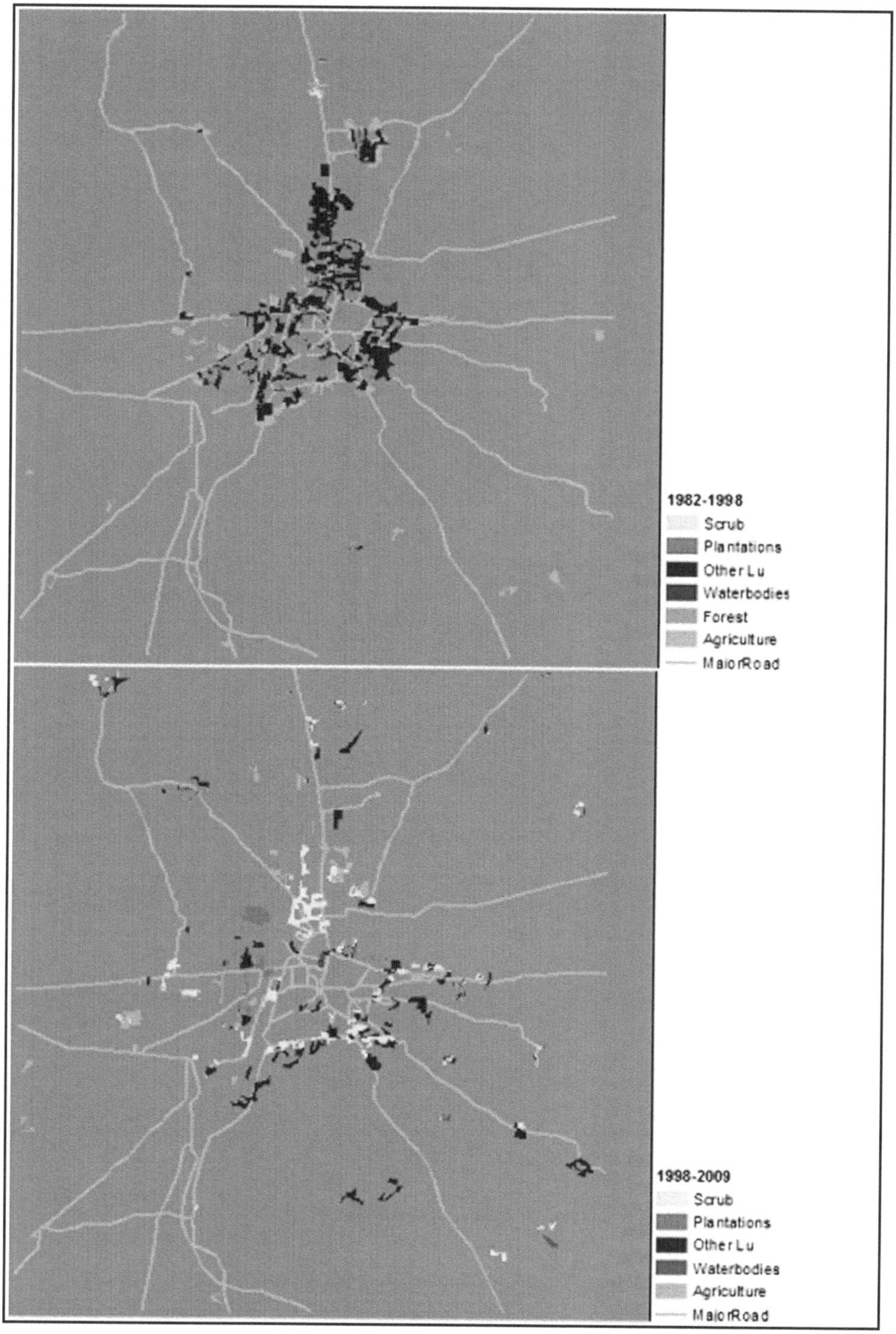

Fig. 6.5: Land-use Categories Converted to Settlements

Fig. 6.6: Land-use Categories Converted to Settlements during 1982-2009

Table 6.4: Land-use/Land-cover Categories Converted to Settlements

Category	1982-1998 (ha)	Percentage (%)	1998-2002 (ha)	Percentage (%)	1982-2009 (ha)	Percentage (%)
Other Land-use/ Landcover	596.62	72.65	278.08	39.47	947.35	58.28
Agriculture	210.45	25.63	137.77	19.56	373.84	23.00
Scrub	4.75	0.58	229.44	32.57	234.77	14.44
Plantations	0.98	0.12	47.20	6.70	48.30	2.97
Water bodies	4.60	0.56	11.96	1.70	17.12	1.05
Forest	3.80	0.46	0.00	0.00	4.26	0.26
Total	**821.20**	**100.00**	**704.45**	**100.00**	**1625.65**	**100.00**

Summary

The landscape metrics corroborate the phenomena of sprawl. Results indicate that 57 per cent of the city is homogenous with high density built-area at the core of Raichur city. Nearly 1625 ha of land from diverse land-uses have been converted to built-up area.

7

3D MAPPING OF RAICHUR CITY

INTRODUCTION

A map is a visual representation of an area – a symbolic depiction highlighting relationships between elements of that space such as: objects, regions, and themes.[82] In a way, the purpose of the maps is to model reality.[83] To model reality the way it is, it requires us to strive to map what we actually experience. Adding a third dimension (3D) to geographic visualization and GIS can make this possible. And today for the same reason, Google earth is appreciated the most. Currently the need for 3D information is rapidly increasing in various areas of human activities such as: urban planning, cadastre, landscape planning and utility management.

This chapter analyses the landscape of Raichur city to illustrate how the use of 2D and 3D dynamic geo-visualization makes it easier to read, analyse and understand the processes of land transformation.

METHODOLOGY

The GIS database – both maps and attribute data has been used to generate 3D GIS. For the DTM (Digital Terrain Model), contours from SOI (Survey of India) have been digitized in ArcGIS and the elevation values have been assigned as z value (Figure 7.1). These contours, 2D line features have been used for generating TIN (Triangulated Irregular Network) using

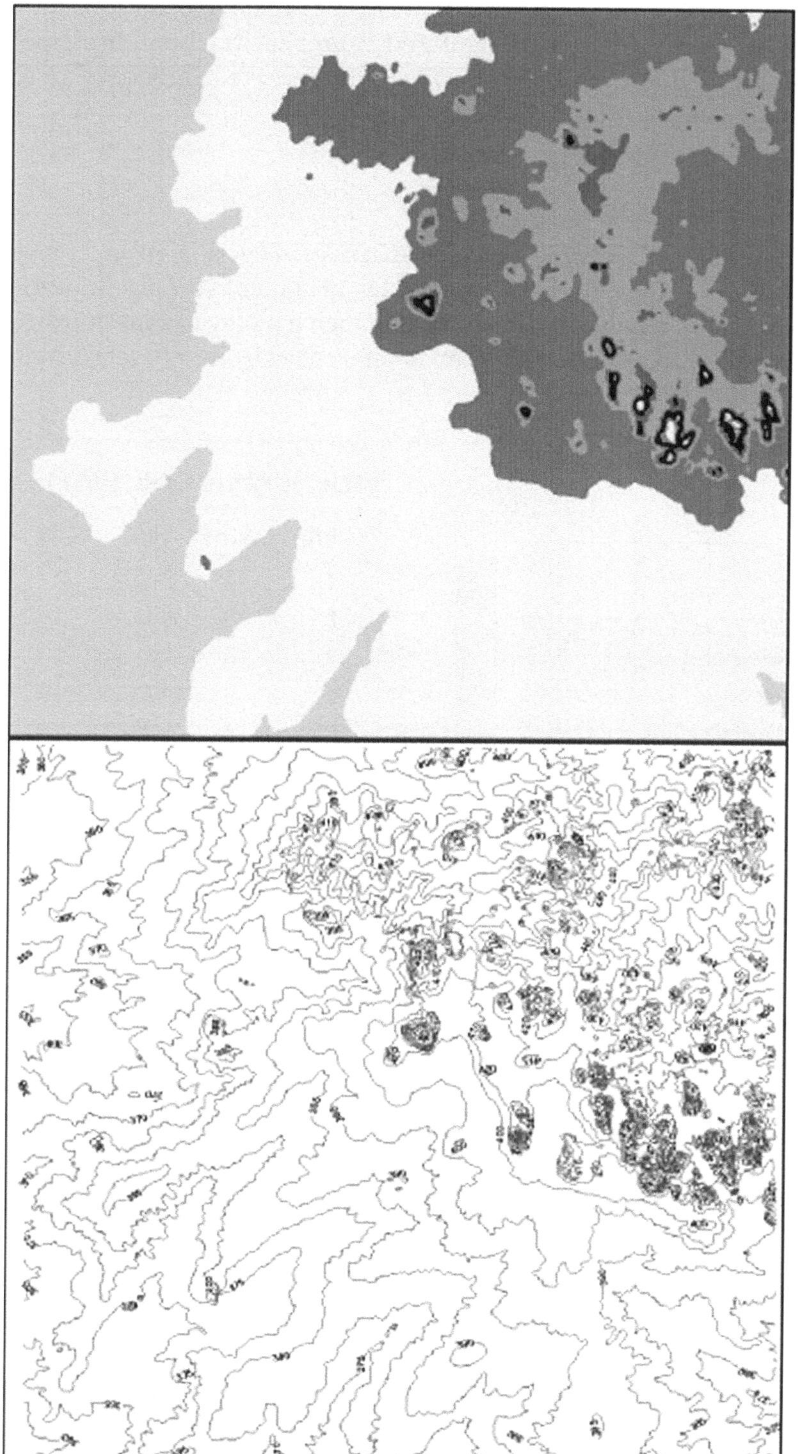

Fig. 7.1: On the Left, Contours Extracted from SOI Toposheet as 2D Line Features with 10 m Contour Interval; on the Right, TIN, A Raster Grid Generated from the 2D Contours using 3D Analyst

3D Analyst. The individual properties of Ward No. 11 have been extruded based on the attribute information collated from the Raichur Municipal Council database. 3D animation video files were created in ArcScene to illustrate the 3D view of ground terrain.

RESULTS AND DISCUSSION

Generating Elevation Grid

The grid defines geographic space as an array of equally sized square grid points arranged in rows and columns. Each grid point stores a numeric value that represents a geographic attribute (such as: elevation or surface slope) for that unit of space. Each grid cell is referenced by its x, y coordinate location (Figure 7.2).

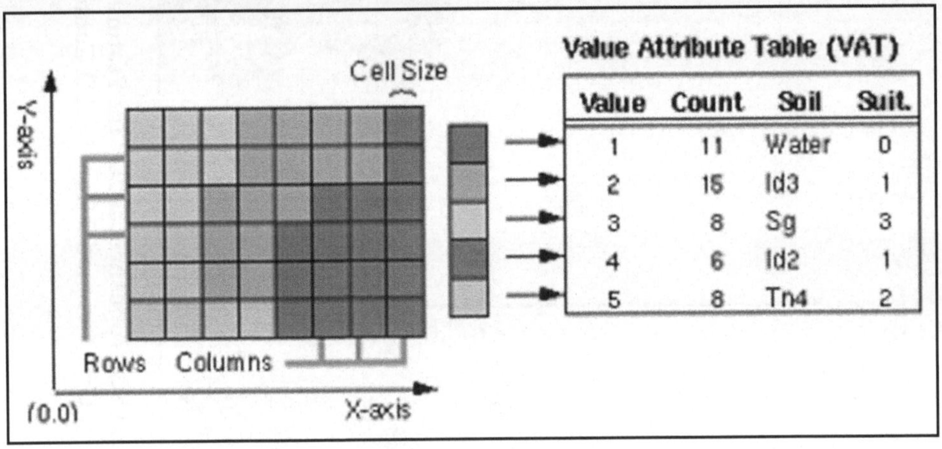

Value	Count	Soil	Suit.
1	11	Water	0
2	15	Id3	1
3	8	Sg	3
4	6	Id2	1
5	8	Tn4	2

Fig. 7.2: Illustration of how Data is Stored in a Grid

In the case of Raichur city, the 2D contour features were digitized in ArcGIS. These 2D features were used for generating TIN (triangulated irregular network) grid (Figure 7.3). TIN is a vector data structure that partitions geographic space into contiguous, non-overlapping triangles. The vertices of each triangle are sample data points with x-, y-, and z-values. These sample points are connected by lines to form Delaunay triangles. TINs are used to store and display surface models.

Digital Terrain Model (DTM)

DTM is interchangeably used with DEM (Digital Elevation Model). DTM refers to a model of reality which includes information relating to factors such as: surface texture as well as elevation.

Location specific design projects benefit from an understanding and representation of the local terrain. Terrain data can be converted into useful

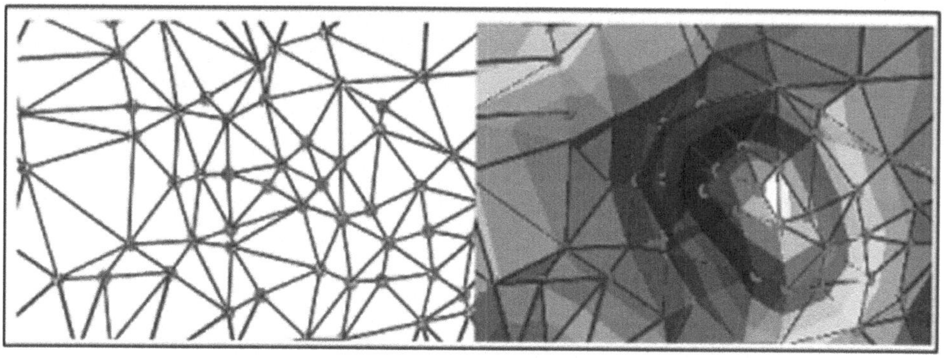

Fig. 7.3: Illustration of the Structure of TIN

representations that may be used in GIS and also popular CAD and 3D modelling formats.

Digital terrain Model of Raichur city has been illustrated in Figure 7.4 with the ward boundaries overlaid as soft fill. An overview of DTM of Raichur reveals that highest altitudes were found at the southeast corner of the area in an inverted 'U' shape along the border of the wards 2,3,13 18 and 21 (Figure 7.5, 7.6, 7.7 and Table 7.1). The terrain undulates from the highest elevation of 520 m on the southeast to 355 m towards north and northwest.

Ward 13, 18 and 21 had highest altitudes with values ranging above 410 m. The lowest altitudes were identified in the ward 33 with an altitude of 355 to 373 m.

Slope Analysis

Slope identifies the steepest downhill slope for a location on a surface. Slope is calculated for each triangle in TINs (Triangulated Irregular Network) and for each cell in rasters. For a TIN, this is the maximum rate of change in elevation across each triangle. For rasters, it is the maximum rate of change in elevation over each cell and its eight neighbours. The lower the slope value, the flatter the terrain; the higher the slope value, the steeper the terrain. The output slope raster can be calculated as per cent slope or degree of slope. When the slope angle equals 45 degrees, the rise is equal to the run. Expressed as a percentage, the slope of this angle is 100 per cent. As the slope approaches vertical (90 degrees), the percentage slope approaches infinity.

The slope function is most frequently run on an elevation grid, as the following Figure 7.8 (b) shows. Steeper slopes are shaded red on the output slope map.

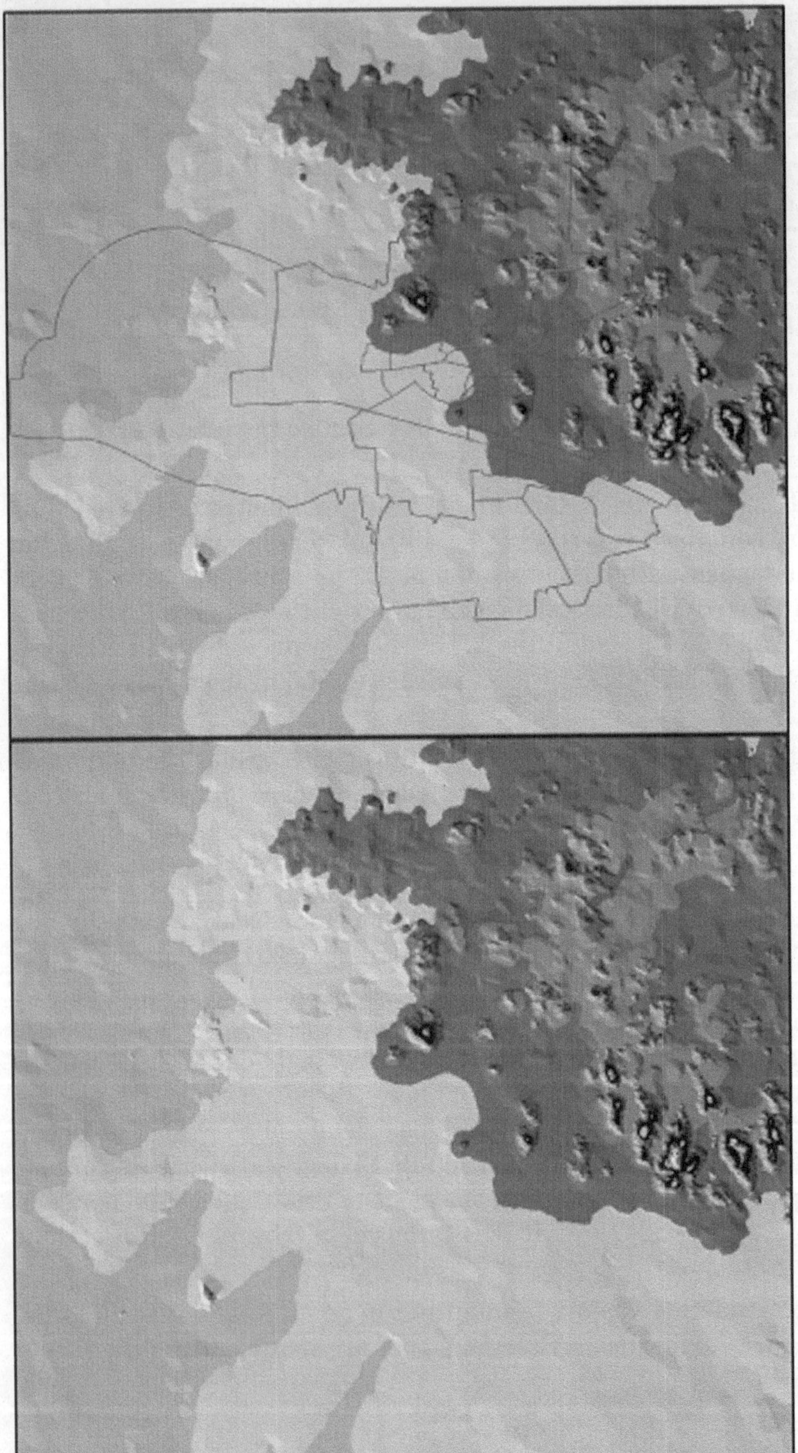

Fig. 7.4: On the Left, TIN with Z unit Conversion of 3.281 Units; on the Right, TIN Overlaid with ward Boundaries using Soft-Line Fill

Table 7.1: Ward-wise Elevation Categories

Elevation (m)	Area (sq. km.)	Area (%)
355-373	7.5	13
373-391	23.9	42
391-410	16.3	28
> 410	8.9	15

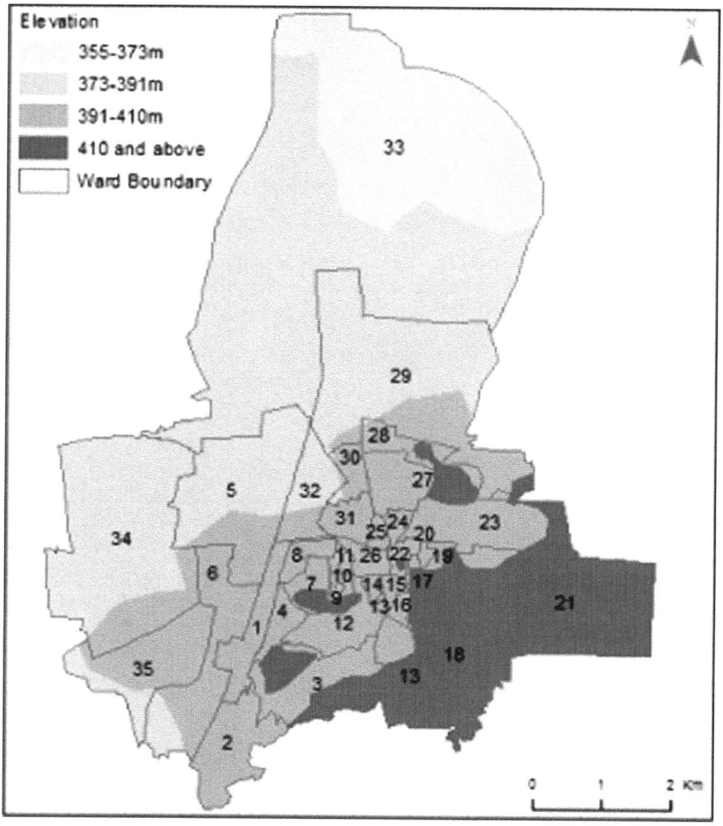

Fig. 7.5: Thematic Map Representing the Elevation Categories Ward-wise

In the case of Raichur city, the slope analysis was performed as degree of slope. Figure 7.8 (b) reveals that most of the terrain in the north and northwest has slope ranging between 0.8-3 indicating that the terrain is predominantly flat. The steepest slope was identified in the hilly terrain located in the southeast part of the city with values ranging from 6-55 degrees.

Fig. 7.6: Digital Terrain Model of Raichur City: Face Elevation with Graduated Colour Ramp

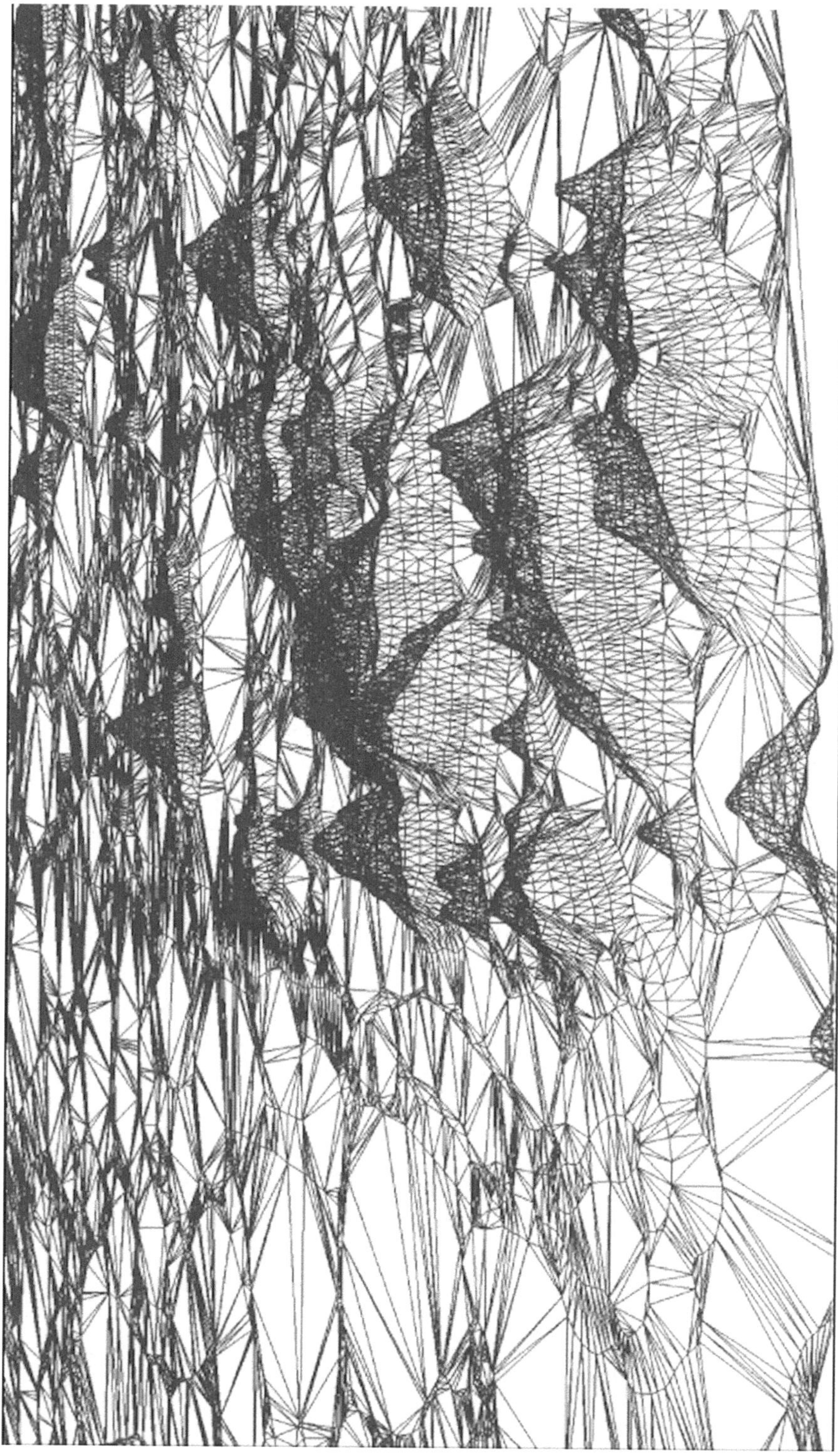

Fig. 7.7: Digital Terrain Model of Raichur City: Edges with Similar Colour Symbol

Aspect Analysis

Aspect is the direction that a slope faces. It identifies the steepest down slope direction at a location on a surface. It can be thought of as slope direction or the compass direction a hill faces. Aspect is calculated for each triangle in TINs and for each cell in rasters. Aspect is measured counter clockwise in degrees from 0 (due north) to 360 (again due north, coming full circle). The value of each cell in an aspect grid indicates the direction in which the cell's slope faces. Flat slopes have no direction and are given a value of -1.

There are many reasons for using the aspect function, such as:

- Find all north facing slopes on a mountain as part of a search for the best slopes for ski runs.
- Calculate the solar illumination for each location in a region as part of a study to determine the diversity of life at each site.
- Find all southerly slopes in a mountainous region to identify locations where the snow is likely to melt first as part of a study to identify those residential locations that are likely to be hit by runoff first.
- Identify areas of flat land to find an area for a plane to land in case of emergency.

The Figure 7.8 (a) shows an input elevation grid and the output aspect grid is Figure 7.8 (d). The aspect analysis indicates that large tracts of land have the aspect direction towards north and northeast. Thus, these areas are likely to be waterlogged during rainy seasons.

Hill Shade Analysis

By modelling shade, the local illumination can be calculated to know whether the cell falls in a shadow or not.

By modelling shadow, the cells that will be in the shadow of another cell at a particular time of day can be identified. Cells that are in the shadow of another cell are coded 0; all other cells are coded with integers from 1 to 255. It's possible to reclassify all the values greater than 1 to 1, producing a binary output raster.

Figure 7.8(c), indicates that some portions of the wards 3, 4, 7, 12, 21, 27, and 28 having hillocks are shaded in black.

Profile Graph

Once the DTM has been created, profile analysis for a region along a path can be viewed as profile graph (Figure 7.9). The figure clearly indicates the steep slope from south to north.

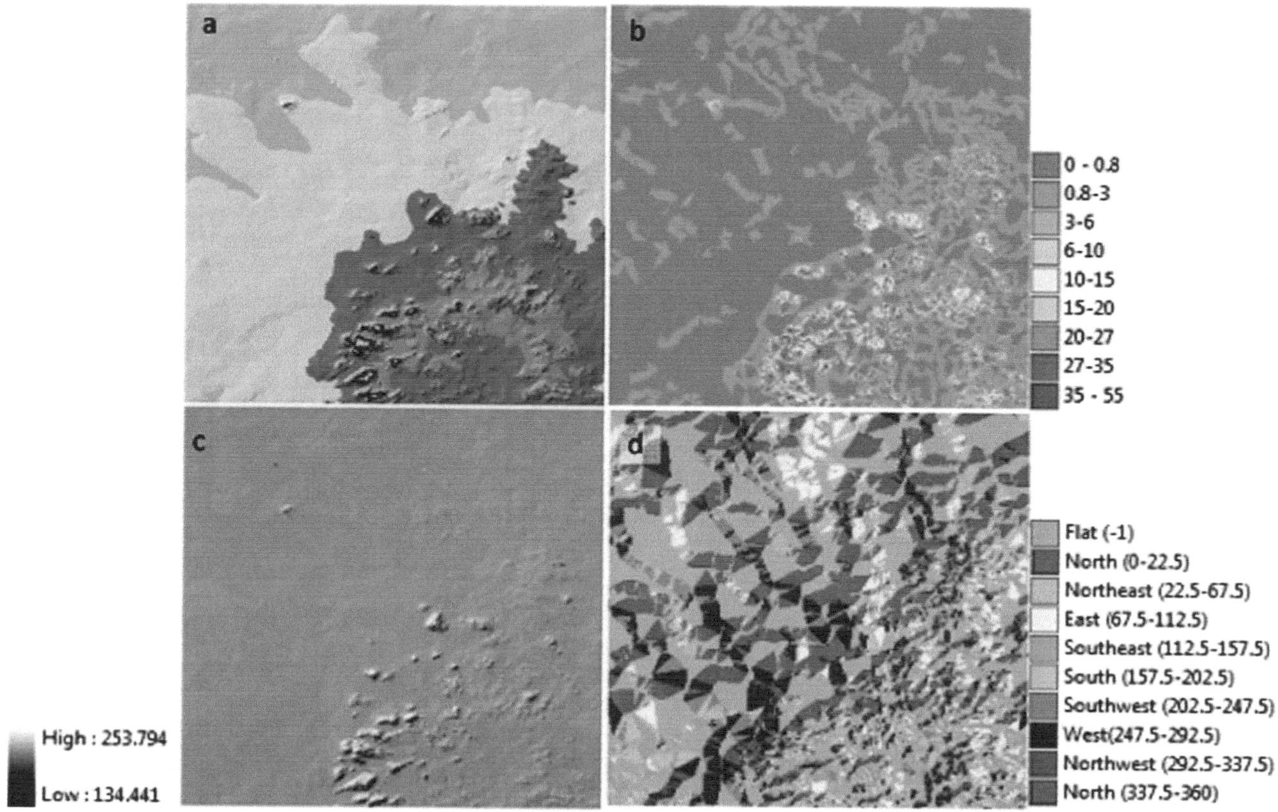

Fig. 7.8: *(a)*: Digital Terrain Model (DTM) of Raichur City
7.8 *(b)*: Slope Analysis Calculates as Degrees
7.8 *(c)*: Hill - shade Analysis of Raichur Surroundings
7.8 *(d)*: Aspect Analysis Performed on the DTM

View-Shed Analysis

View-shed is useful to know how visible objects might be – for example: from which locations on the landscape will the water towers be visible if they are placed in this location, and what will the view be, like from this road?

View-shed identifies the cells in an input raster that can be seen from one or more observation points or lines. Each cell in the output raster receives a value that indicates how many observer points can be seen from each location. If there is only one observer point, as illustrated in Figure 7.10 each cell that can see that observer point is given a value of 1. All cells that cannot see the observer point are given a value of 0. The observer points feature class can contain points or lines.

In the example mentioned in Figure 7.10, the view-shed from an observation tower is identified as person standing on the ground at 77°21'0.517"E and 16°12'56.832"N. The elevation raster displays the height of the land (white colour locations represent lower elevations), and the observer location is marked as person standing. The height of the observation tower can be specified in the analysis; in this case it is taken as 2 meters. Cells in the white are visible from the observation point, and cells in pink are not visible.

Displaying a hill-shade underneath the elevation and the output from the Viewshed function is a useful technique for visualizing the relationship between visibility and terrain. Not only one can determine which cells can be seen from the observation tower, if there are several observation points, it also enables to determine which observers can see each observed location. Knowing which observer can see which locations can affect decision-making. For example, in a visual quality study for citing a landfill it may be determined that the proposed landfill's location is favourable if it can only be seen from dirty roads and not from the primary and secondary roads.

Multimedia GIS

Once the DTM for Raichur has been generated, using Arcscene, key frames were created and exported to video file using Cinepak Codec by Radius with compression ratio of 91 per cent, with keyframe every 20 frames. A snapshot of a few key frames has been illustrated as Figure 7.11 and 7.12.

SUMMARY

In this chapter, various aspects of 3D mapping – slope, aspect, hill shade, and view-shed analyses were studied to understand the digital terrain model of the city. Also multimedia GIS were created using ARCScene and 3D analyst.

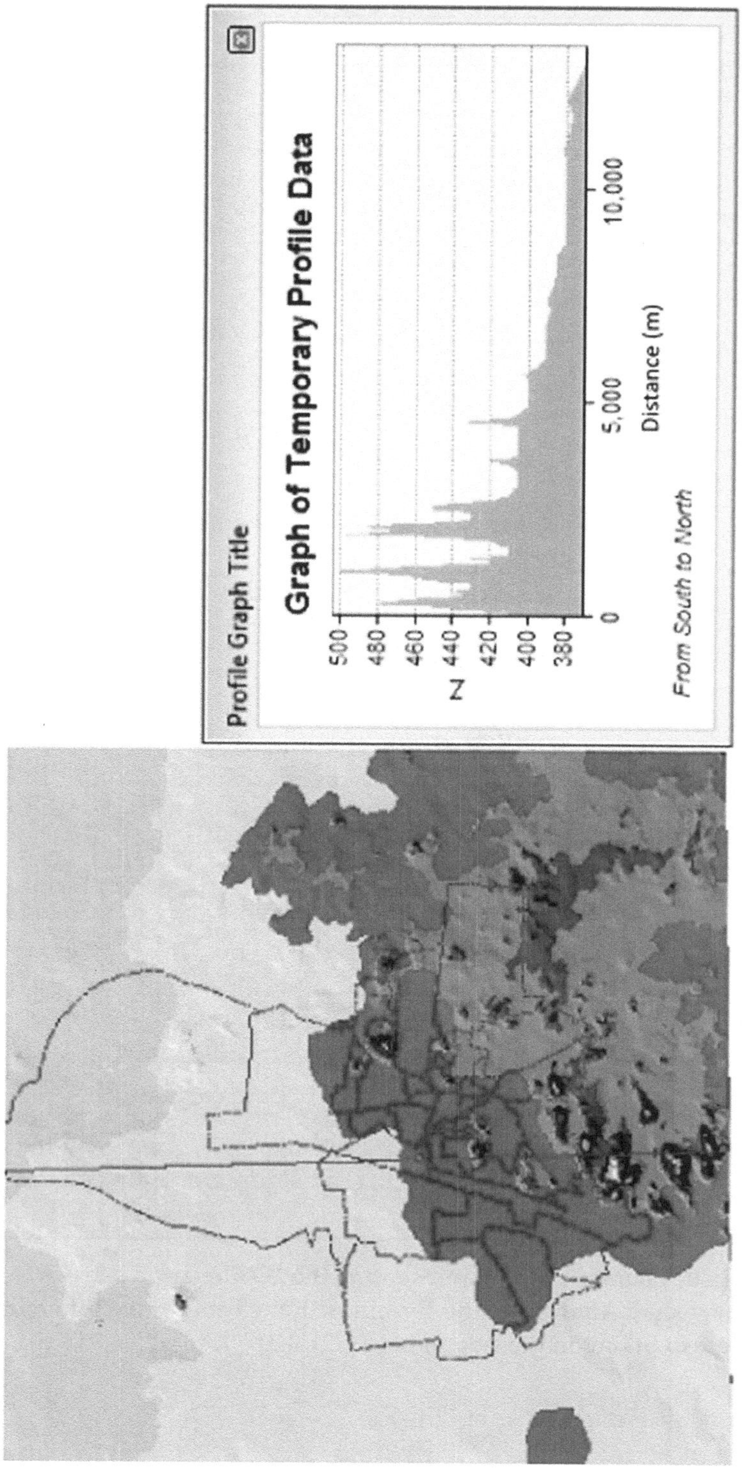

Fig.7.9: On the Left, 3D Elevation with the Line of Path (Marked in Blue). On the Right, Profile Analysis Plotted along the Path with Respect to the Ground Elevation (Z, in Meters)

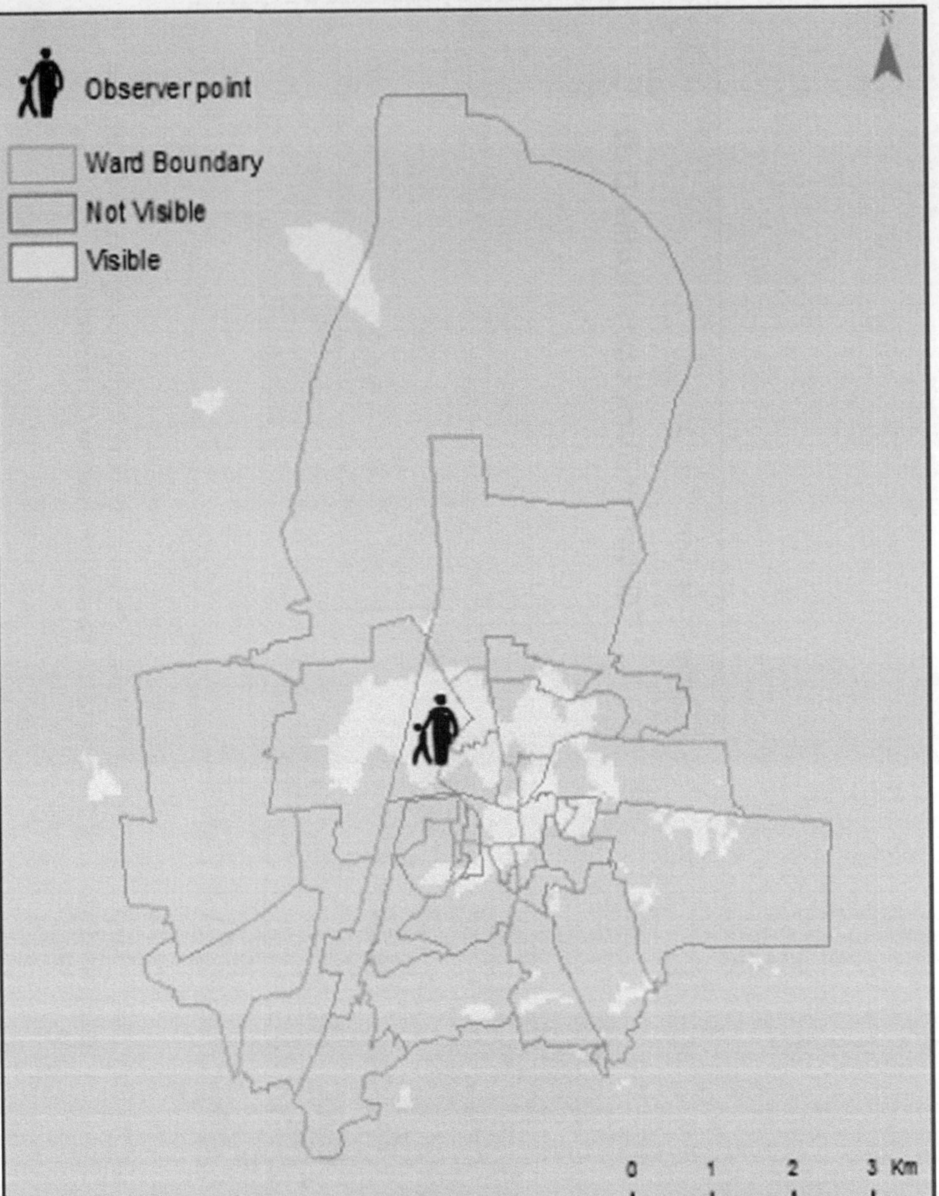

Fig. 7.10: On the Left, Thematic Map Representing the 2D Elevation Ward-wise. On the Right, View-shed Analysis of the Terrain with the Perspective Wherein if a Person were to Stand on the Ground at 77°21′0.517″E 16°12′56.832″N

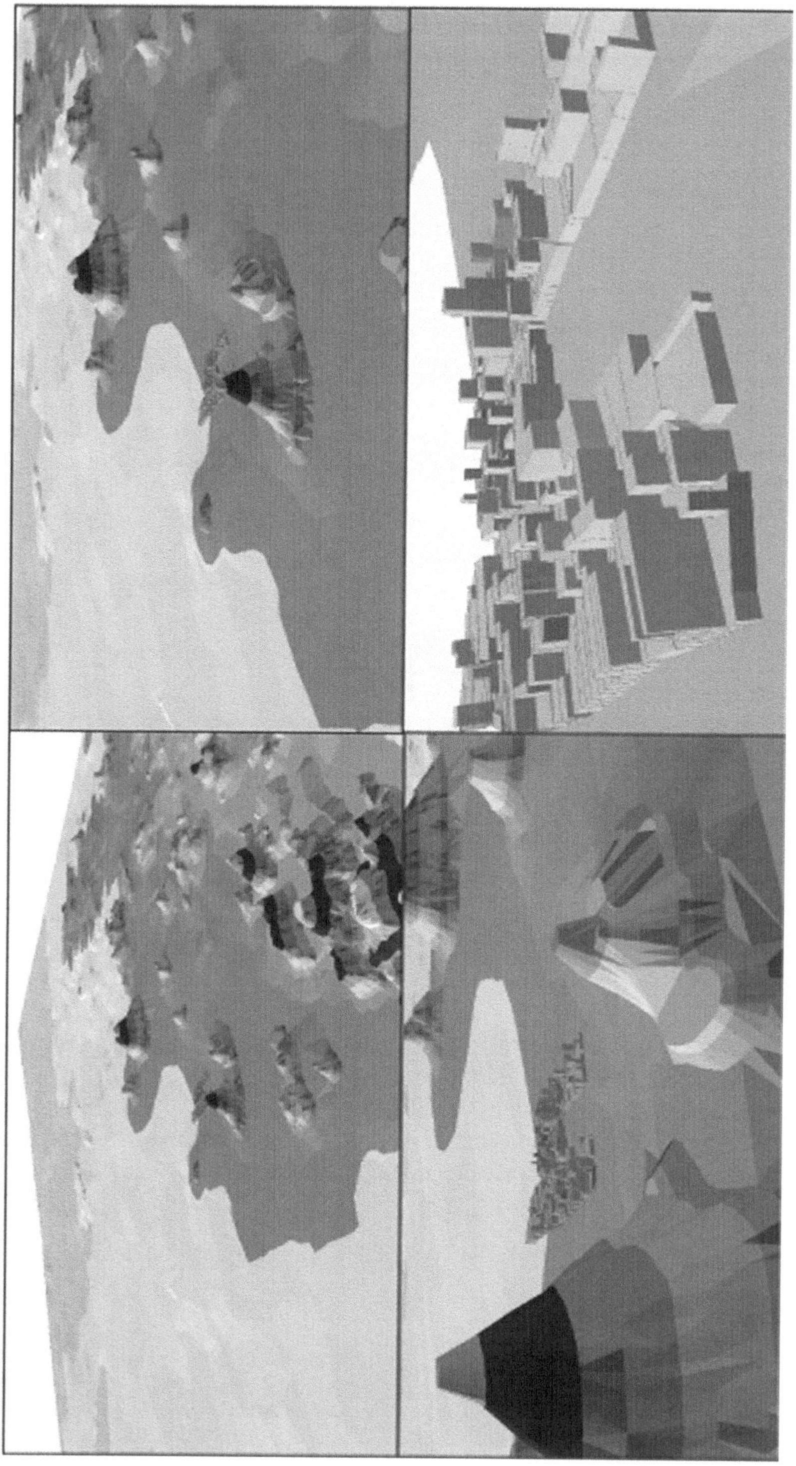

Fig. 7.11: Snapshots of the DTM Showing the 3D Extrusion of Buildings of Ward No. 11

Fig. 7.12: Close View of the 3D Extrusion of Buildings of Ward No. 11 using the Vector Layer of Individual Property

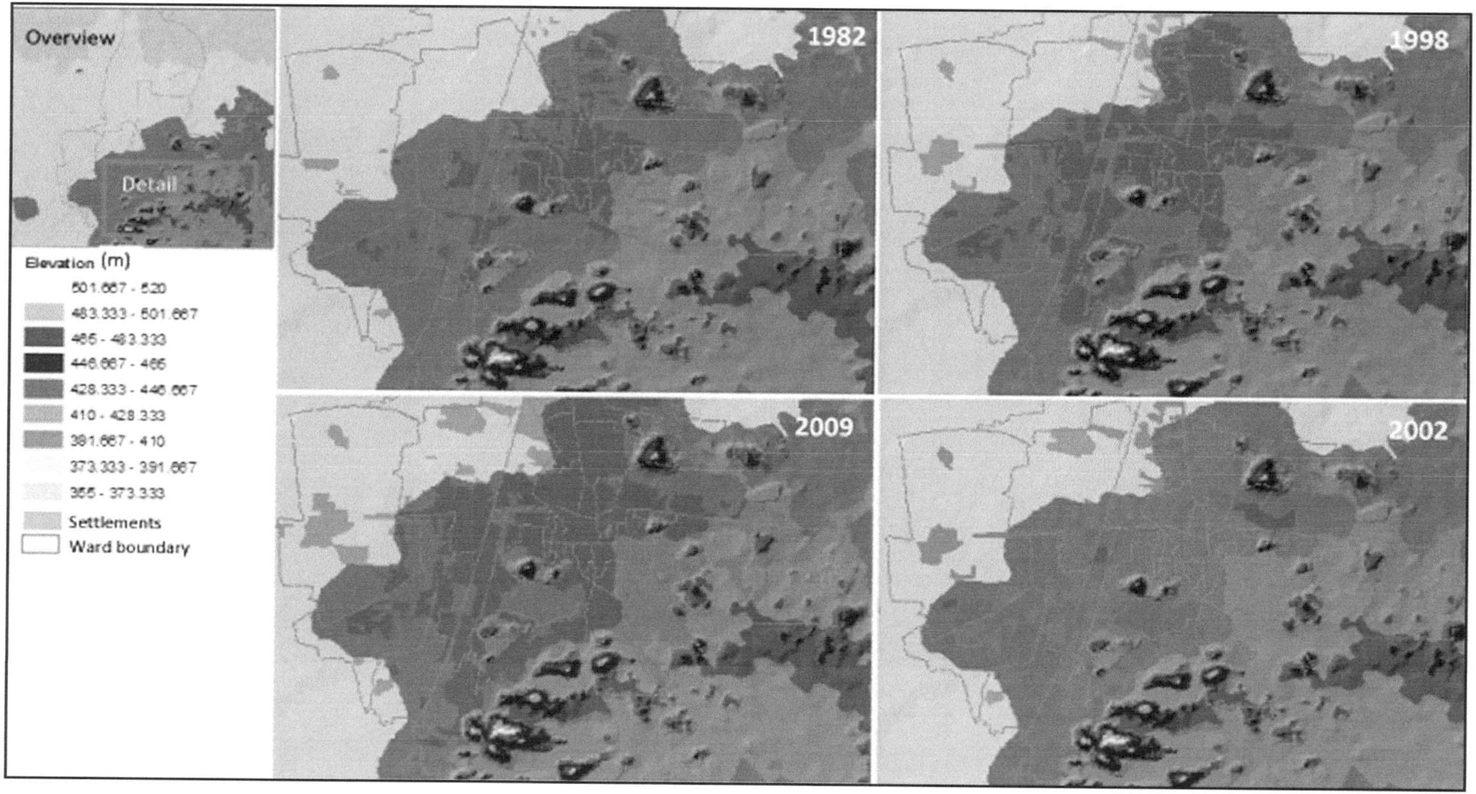

Fig. 7.13: The Spread of Built-up Area in the Southeast Part of the City, Notwithstanding the Presence of Hillocks in this Region

The DTM models indicate that the hillocks in the southeast corner of the city could act as potential barriers in containing the sprawl. However, between 2002 and 2009 there had been frantic real estate development because of which vast stretches of hillocks are levelled in the southeast part of city (Figure 7.13). On the contrary, the much prospective areas with flat terrain in the northeast area falling in wards 5, 29, 32, 33 and 34 are occupied by low income groups and slums. These lands are purchased as investments rather than for real-estate development.

8

DEVELOPING A VERSATILE, MULTI-UTILITY WEB GIS FOR RAICHUR CITY

RAICHUR E-CITY

INTRODUCTION

GIS provides valuable information that is required for the government, the urban and regional planners to take critical decisions towards mitigating the undesirable impacts of urban sprawl.[84] Implementing a web-based GIS database is the best way to provide access to the GIS data.[85]

Web GIS enables publishing of maps online and help citizens understand the proposed development plans. Informing the public, receiving input, and garnering support for development initiatives improves the ability to serve the community.

In an endeavour to foster data creation and sharing; visualizing and analysing data; and delivering that information to office staff, field crews, and decision-makers, the GIS database of Raichur city has been designed and presented as web GIS. This software application named *'Raichur e-City'*, has been developed using free and open source software (FOSS).

Free open source software (FOSS) has gained immense popularity in recent times.[86] Open source license guarantees freedom to read, redistribute, modify and use the software freely.

ARCHITECTURE OF RAICHUR E-CITY

Raichur e-City (ReC), has been developed using the logistics of open system architecture: *Mapserver, Apache and html web browser* (Figure 8.1).

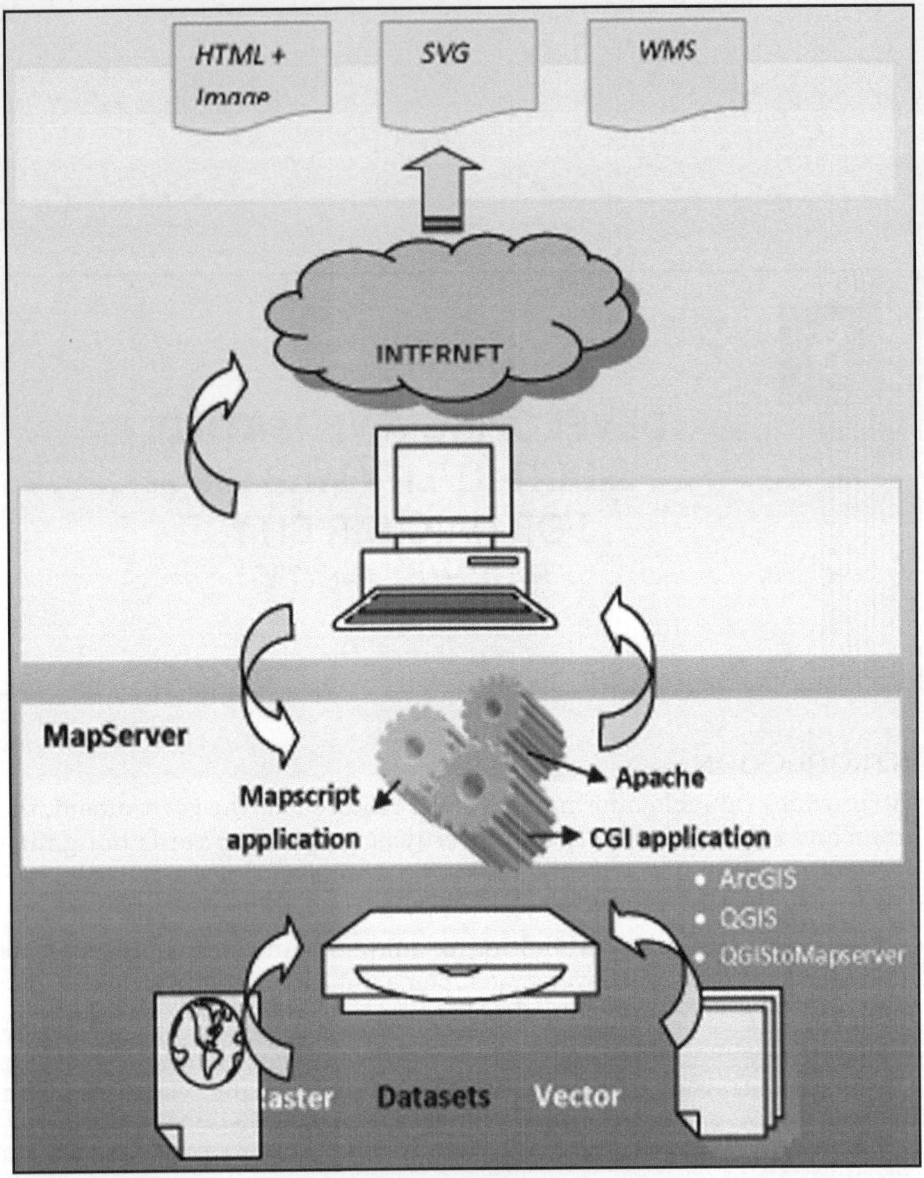

Fig. 8.1: Architecture of *Raichur e-City* web GIS Application

Raichur e-City is an OGC – WMS (Open GIS Consortium Web Map Service) complaint, which is capable of serving large-scale GIS database on the web. Apart from being a web solution, this prototype can also be used as a stand alone GIS system.

GIS Data Preparation

The spatial data has been created and integrated with the non-spatial data using ArcGIS 9.2 desktop GIS software. A list of the vector layers that has been used in web GIS application has been presented in Table 8.1. The source of these data sets, both spatial and non-spatial has been presented in detail in chapter 3.

Table 8.1: Details of the Vector Layers used in Web GIS Application

Feature	File Name	Feature Class
Ward boundaries	Ward Boundary Polygon.shp	Polygon
Block boundaries	Block Boundary Polygon.shp	Polygon
Locality boundaries	Localities Polygon.shp	Polygon
Water bodies	Water bodies.shp	Polygon
Contours	Contours.shp	Polyline
Elevation categories	Elevation Analysis.shp	Polygon
Infrastructure details	Infra_Points.shp	Points
Infrastructure details	Infra_Polygon.shp	Polygon
Property details	Property.shp	Polygon
Property details	Property_Ward11_Block1.shp	Polygon
Major roads	Major Road.shp	Polyline
Other roads	Other Roads.shp	Polyline
Railway line	Railway.shp	Polyline
Landuse/landcover categories for year 1981	LuLcMap1981.shp	Polygon
Landuse/landcover categories for year 1998	LuLcMap1998.shp	Polygon
Landuse/landcover categories for year 2002	LuLcMap2002.shp	Polygon
Landuse/landcover categories for year 2009	LuLcMap2009.shp	Polygon

MapServer

MapServer is an open source geographic data rendering engine written in C programming language. Beyond browsing GIS data, MapServer allows to create 'geographic image maps', that is, maps that can direct users to the content.[87] For example, the *Raichur e-City* can provide users with more than 10,000 web pages, reports and maps via a single application. The same application also serves as 'map engine' for other portions of the site, providing spatial context where needed.

MapServer was originally developed by the University of Minnesota (UMN) For Net project in co-operation with NASA, and the Minnesota

Department of Natural Resources (MNDNR).[87] Later it was hosted by the TerraSIP project, a NASA sponsored project between the UMN and a consortium of land management interests.

MapServer is now a project of OSGeo, and is maintained by a growing number of developers (nearing 20) from around the world. It is supported by a diverse group of organizations that fund enhancements and maintenance, and administered within OSGeo by the MapServer *Project Steering Committee* made up of developers and other contributors.

Some of the salient features of MapServer are:

- Advanced cartographic output.
  - o scale dependent feature drawing and application execution;
  - o feature labelling including label collision mediation;
  - o fully customizable, template driven output;
  - o truetype fonts;
  - o map element automation (scalebar, reference map, and legend);
  - o thematic mapping using logical- or regular expression-based classes;
- Support for popular scripting and development environments.
  - o PHP, Python, Perl, Ruby, Java, and .NET;
- Cross-platform support.
  - o linux, Windows, Mac OS X, Solaris, and more;
- Support of numerous *Open Geospatial Consortium* (OGC) standards.
  - o WMS (client/server), non-transactional WFS (client/server), WMC, WCS, Filter Encoding, SLD, GML, SOS, OM;
- A multitude of raster and vector data formats.
  - o TIFF/GeoTIFF, EPPL7, and many others via GDAL;
  - o ESRI shapefiles, PostGIS, ESRI ArcSDE, Oracle Spatial, MySQL and many others via OGR;
- Map projection support.
  - o on-the-fly map projection with 1000s of projections through the Proj.4 library.

In its most basic form, MapServer is a *CGI* programme that sits inactive on the Web server. When a request is sent to MapServer, it uses information passed in the request URL and the *Mapfile* to create an image of the requested map. The request may also return images for legends, scale bars, reference maps, and values passed as CGI variables.

MapServer can be extended and customized through *MapScript* or *templating*. It can be built to support many different *vector* and *raster* input data formats, and it can generate a multitude of *output* formats. Most pre-compiled MapServer distributions contain most of its features.

A simple MapServer application consists of:

- *Map File*: A structured text configuration file for the MapServer application. It defines the area of the map, tells the MapServer programme where the data is and where to output images. It also defines the map layers, including their data source, projections, and symbology. It must have a *map* extension or MapServer will not recognize it.
- *Geographic Data*: MapServer can utilize many geographic data source types. The default format is the ESRI shape file. Many other data formats can be supported.
- *HTML Pages*: The interface between the user and MapServer. They normally sit in web root. In its simplest form, MapServer can be called to place a static map image on a html page. To make the map interactive, the image is placed in an html form on a page.

CGI programmes are 'stateless', every request they get is new and they don't remember anything about the last time that they were hit by the application. For this reason, every time the application sends a request to MapServer, it needs to pass context information (what layers are on, where you are on the map, application mode, etc.,) in hidden form variables or URL variables.

A simple MapServer *CGI* application may include two html pages:

- *Initialization File:* Uses a form with hidden variables to send an initial query to the http server and MapServer. This form could be placed on another page or be replaced by passing the initialization information as variables in a URL.
- *Template File:* Controls how the maps and legends output by MapServer will appear in the browser. By referencing MapServer CGI variables in the template html, you allow MapServer to populate them with values related to the current state of the application (*e.g.,* map image name, reference image name, map extent, etc.,) as it creates the html page for the browser to read. The template also determines how the user can interact with the MapServer application (browse, zoom, pan, and query).
- *MapServer CGI*: The binary or executable file that receives requests and returns images, data, etc. It sits in the cgi-bin or scripts directory of the http server. The Web server user must have execute rights for the directory that it sits in, and for security reasons, it should not be in the web root. By default, this programme is called *mapserv*.

- *HTTP Server*: Serves up the html pages when hit by the user's browser. This needs a working HTTP (Web) server, such as: Apache or Microsoft Internet Information Server, on the machine on which you are installing MapServer. In the case of *Raichur e-City* Apache has been used.

MapFile Creation

Mapfile is an essential component for MapServer to render the vector and raster layers. The mapfile for *Raichur e-city* has been created using a combination of *Quantum GIS (QGIS)* and *QGISToMapserver* tool.

QGIS is a user friendly Open Source Geographic Information System (GIS) that runs on Linux, Unix, Mac OSX, and Windows. QGIS supports vector, raster, and database formats. QGIS is licensed under the GNU Public License[88] (Figure 8.2).

QgisToMapServer converts a saved QGIS project file to a map file, ready to be served with MapServer. This makes QGIS a powerful editor for creating map files.[89]

The typical process used for creating map file for Raichur e-City:

1. Load the required layers into QGIS.
2. Symbolize each layer, setting colour, styles, etc.
3. Save the QGIS project.
4. Run qgistomapserver.
5. Select a name for the map file.
6. Select the name of the saved project file.
7. Set other options for export.
8. Export the file.

QgisToMapServer works with project files created with QGIS version 0.9 or greater.

Apache http SeRver

The Apache HTTP Server, commonly referred to as Apache, is web server software notable for playing a key role in the initial growth of the World Wide Web. In 2009 it became the first web server software to surpass the 100 million website milestone.[65] Apache was the first viable alternative to the Netscape Communications Corporation web server (currently known as Oracle iPlanet Web Server), and has since evolved to rival other web servers in terms of functionality and performance. Typically Apache is run on a Unix-like operating system.[76]

Apache is developed and maintained by an open community of developers under the auspices of the Apache Software Foundation. The

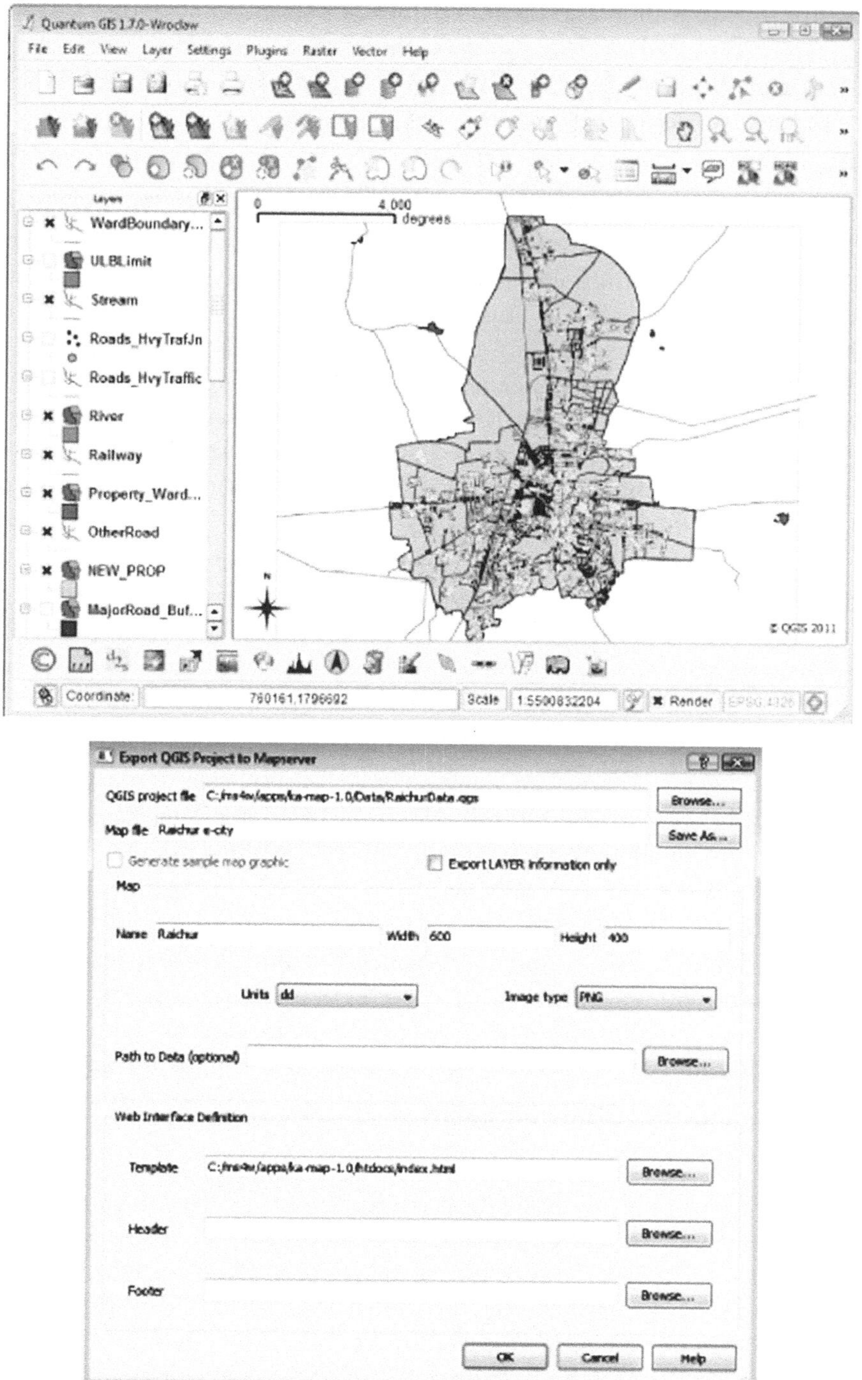

Fig. 8.2: QGIS Interface for Data Representation (above); using the QGIStoMapserver Tool for Generating the Mapfile

application is available for a wide variety of operating systems, including Unix, GNU, FreeBSD, Linux, Solaris, Novell NetWare, AmigaOS, Mac OS X, Microsoft Windows, OS/2, TPF, and eComStation. Released under the Apache License, Apache is open-source software.

Features

Apache supports a variety of features, many implemented as compiled modules which extend the core functionality. These can range from server-side programming language support to authentication schemes. Some common language interfaces support Perl, Python, Tcl, and PHP. Popular authentication modules include mod_access, mod_auth, mod_digest, and mod_auth_digest, the successor to mod_digest. A sample of other features include SSL and TLS support (mod_ssl), a proxy module (mod_proxy), a URL rewriter (also known as a rewrite engine, implemented under mod_rewrite), custom log files (mod_log_config), and filtering support (mod_include and mod_ext_filter).

Popular compression methods on Apache include the external extension module, mod_gzip, implemented to help with reduction of the size (weight) of web pages served over HTTP. ModSecurity is an open source intrusion detection and prevention engine for web applications. Apache logs can be analyzed through a web browser using free scripts such as: AWStats/W3Perl or Visitors.

Virtual hosting allows one Apache installation to serve many different actual websites. For example, one machine with one Apache installation could simultaneously serve www.example.com, www.test.com, test47.test-server.test.com, etc.

Apache features configurable error messages, DBMS-based authentication databases, and content negotiation. It is also supported by several graphical user interfaces (GUIs). It also supports password authentication and digital certificate authentication. Apache has a built in search engine and an HTML authorizing tool and supports FTP.

Other Components of Raichur e-City

Web Client

The web client is an application environment, which runs on the user's site, including state of application in a web browser environment. No application session is conserved on the server site. The Web services ensure data access. All web client communication comes via HTTP(S) protocol. The Web GIS of *Raichur e-city* is powered by *Ka-Map 1.0* which can be accessed by any html browser such as: Internet Explorer, Mozilla Firefox, Opera or Chrome.

About Ka-Map. Ka-Map is an open source project that is aimed at providing a javascript API for developing highly interactive web-mapping interfaces using features available in modern web browsers.[90]

Ka-Map has a number of interesting features. It sports the following user interface elements such as:

- Interactive, continuous panning without reloading the page.
- Keyboard navigation options (zooming, panning).
- Zooming to pre-set scales.
- Scalebar, legend and keymap support.
- optional layer control on client side (layers are made visible instantly but at reduced performance due to more images, and potentially slower browser interactivity).

Web

The Web service with REST interface ensures all HTTP(S) communications of the Web GIS Client with Server Object extended MapServer type. Communication of the web application comes through ArcGIS Server Object Manager (SOM) components via DCOM. Authentication performs on REST web layer of applicant services ArcGIS Server interface with token services.

Server

Server Object extension of MapServer type performs on data operation like: as spatial and attributes selects, relace passing, attributes edits, creation of new objects – redline.

Underlying map services make use the technique of map cache for ensured fast reaction over data portrayal, layers configuration for attribute searching and data editing.

Web services present data file and largely application logic. Web services run at ArcGIS Server environment. Dynamic map services used optimalized portrayal core of ArcGIS Server for viewing data.

Data operation such as: attribute tasks, spatial tasks and data edits ensured extention of ArcGIS Server map service. This is an extention functionality of Server Object MapServer type, which enables full-value access for properties of ArcSDE geodatabase (relations, domains, data edits) for application.

Users Environment

Any computer with internet connection or standalone system with Raichur-GIS installed would enable the user to explore and analyse Raichur GIS database.

Requirements for Users

For user application any web browser (Mozilla Firefox, IE, Chrome, Opera, etc.,) and plug-in of web browser Adobe Flash Player 9.0.115 (eventually upper) is required.

Advantages

- Openness in solution – access through web interface.
- Easy specific applications according to users requirements.
- Safer access.
- Widely accessible data format.
- Integration with advanced logic commonly reserved only for 'thick' clients.
- Integration with others ERP and CRM systems.
- Coherent and complex view on data.
- Decrease of administrative costs.
- Less requirements on server (server works as file server and not as application server).

CODE DESIGN

Mapfile

The *mapfile* is the basic configuration file for data access and styling for MapServer. As mentioned earlier, the mapfile for *Raichur e-city* was generated using QGIS and QGIStoMapserver tool.

The mapfile is an ASCII text file, and is made up of different objects. Each object has a variety of parameters available for it. All *mapfile* (or mapfile) parameters are documented in the mapfile reference. The sample mapfile example has been presented here for a few vector layers:

****

```
Map
Name RGIS
# Map image size
Size 600 400
Units dd
Extent 738008.763400 1788996.009855 765325.396185 1801617.143942
Projection
'proj=longlat'
'ellps=WGS84'
'towgs84=0,0,0,0,0,0,0'
'no_defs'
End
```

```
# Background colour for the map canvas — change as desired
Image colour 255 255 255
Image Quality 95
Image Type PNG
Output Format
Name 'PNG'
Driver 'GD/PNG'
Mime Type 'Image/PNG'
# Image Mode PC256
Extension 'PNG'
End
# Legend
Legend
Image colour 255 255 255
Status on
Key Size 18 12
Label
Type Bitmap
Size Medium
Colour 0 0 89
End
# Web interface definition. Only the template parameter
# is required to display a map. See MapServer documentation
Web
# Set Image Path to the path where MapServer should
# write its output.
Image Path '/tmp/'
# Set Image URL to the url that points to Image Path
# as defined in your web server configuration
Image URL '/tmp/'
# WMS server settings
Meta Data
'wms_title' 'RGIS'
'wms_onlineresource' 'http://my.host.com/cgi-
bin/mapserv?map=wms.mapand'
'wms_srs' 'EPSG:4326'
End
```

#Scale range at which web interface will operate
Template and header/footer settings
Only the template parameter is required to display a map. See MapServer documentation
Template 'C:/ms4w/apps/ka-map-1.0/htdocs/index.html'
End

****

Map Object

Map
Name RGIS
Map Image Size
Size 600 400
Units dd
Extent 738008.763400 1788996.009855 765325.396185 1801617.143942
End

#
Extent is the output extent in the units of the output map
Size is the width and height of the map image in pixels
#

Layer Object

MapServer 5.0 and above has no limit to the number of layers to add in a mapfile. The DATA parameter is relative to the SHAPEPATH parameter the MAP object. If no DATA extension is provided in the filename, MapServer will assume it is an ESRI shapefile (shp).

Vector Layers

Vector layers of TYPE point, line, or polygon can be displayed. The following example shows how to display only lines from a TYPE polygon layer, using the OUTLINECOLOUR parameter:

Layer
Name 'LuLcMap1981'
Type Polygon
Data 'C:\ms4w\apps\ka-map-1.0\Data\LuLcMap1981.shp'
Meta Data
'wms_title' 'LuLcMap1981'
End

Status Default

Transparency 100

Projection

'proj=longlat'

'ellps=WGS84'

'towgs84=0,0,0,0,0,0,0'

'no_defs'

End

Class

Name 'LuLcMap1981'

Style

Symbol 0

Size 2

Outline colour 0 0 0

Colour 164 110 66

End

Class and Style Objects

Typical styling information is stored within the Class and Style Objects of a Layer. MapServer 5.0 and above has no limit to the number of classes or styles in a mapfile.

The following example shows how to display a road line with two colours by using overlayed Style objects:

Class

Name 'LuLcMap1981'

Style

Symbol 0

Size 2

Outline colour 0 0 0

Colour 164 110 66

End

Symbols

Symbols can be defined directly in the mapfile, or in a separate file. The separate file method must use the Symbolset parameter in the MAP object, such as:

Class

Name 'LuLcMap1998'

Style

Symbol 0

Size 2

Outline colour 0 0 0

Colour 40 234 241

End

Label

Labels are defined within a Layer object. The Labelitem parameters in the Layer object can be used to label by a specific column in the data refer to a Fontset file, that is set in the Map object, that contains a reference to the available font names An example Label object that references one of the above fonts might look like:

Label

Font 'sans-bold'

Type truetype

Size 10

Position LC

Partials False

Colour 100 100 100

Outline Colour 242 236 230

End

Class Expressions

MapServer supports three types of Class expressions in a Layer:

1. String comparisons.

    (EXPRESSION 'Lu Category')

2. Regular expressions.

    (EXPRESSION /^9 | ^10/)

3. Logical expressions

    ([POPULATION] > 50000 AND '[LANGUAGE]' eq 'FRENCH')

Note: Logical expressions should be avoided wherever possible as they are very costly in terms of drawing time.

Include

MapServer 4.10 and above, any part of the mapfile can be stored in a separate file and added to the main mapfile using the INCLUDE parameter. The filename to be included can have any extension, and it is always relative to the main *map* file. Here are some potential uses:

- Layer s can be stored in files and included to any number of applications.
- Style s can also be stored and included in multiple applications.

The following is an example of using mapfile includes to include a layer definition in a separate file:

If 'shadedrelief.lay' contains:

```
Layer
Name 'shadedrelief'
Status on
Type Raster
Data ' QB_RAICHUR.Tiff'
End
```

therefore the main mapfile would contain:

```
MAP
...
Include "shadedrelief.lay"
...
End
```

The following is an example of a mapfile where all LAYER s are in separate .lay files, and all other objects (Web, Reference, Scalebar, etc.,) are stored in a '.ref' file:

```
Name 'base'
#
# include reference objects
#
Include "../templates/template.ref"
#
# Start of layer definitions
#
```

Include '../layers/RGIS/RGIS_outline.lay'

Include '../layers/ RGIS /base/1m/blocks.lay'

Include '../layers/ RGIS /base/1m/roads_atlas_of_RGIS_1m.lay'

Include '../layers/RGIS/base/1m/roads_atlas_of_RGIS_1m_shields.lay'

Include '../layers/RGIS/base/1m/populated_places.lay'

End

Map File

Getting MapServer Running

A HTTP request can be directly sent to the MapServer CGI programme without passing any configuration variables. For example, typing "http://your.domain.name/cgi-bin/ms4/mapserv.exe" in the web browser returns a message, '*No query information to decode. QUERY_STRING not set.*' This means Mapserver the installation is working.

The Software Package – *'Raichur e-City'*

The software package *'Raichur e-City'* has been designed to perform a full installation of Apache, PHP, MapServer CGI, MapScript (CSharp, Java, PHP, Python), and to provide the capability to install several applications components easily and quickly. The simplest way to do this on Windows is to provide a predetermined directory structure and force everything into that mould.

The directory structure, while fixed within itself, is designed to be somewhat portable. While the ms4w_xxx.zip file needs to be installed at the root of a hard drive, it doesn't have to be the C:/ drive. Moving the package to the root of a different drive is simple – just copy it there. To move it to a subdirectory is more difficult – you'll need to search for /ms4w in all the files and replace it with your new path.

The design also accommodates simple upgrades to the core package and to applications, without affecting the local configuration or the configuration of other installed applications.

Contents of the Software

The following are included in the base package:

- Apache version 2.2.19.
- PHP version 5.3.6.
- MapServer 6.0.1 CGI and MapScript (CSharp, Java, PHP, Python).
- GDAL 1.8.1.
- mapserver utilities.
- gdal/ogr utilities.

- proj.4 utilities.
- shp2tile utility.
- shapelib utilities.
- shpdiff utility.
- avce00 utilities.
- PHP_OGR Extension 1.1.1.
- OWTChart 1.2.0.

MapServer Version Information

MapServer version 6.0.1 Output = GIF Output = PNG Output = JPEG Output = KML Supports = PROJ Supports = AGG Supports = Cairo Supports = Freetype Supports = ICONV Supports = FRIBIDI Supports = WMS_Server Supports = WMS_CLIENT Supports = WFS_Server

Supports = WFS_Client

Supports = WCS_Server Supports = SOS_Server

Supports = FASTCGI Supports = Threads Supports = GEOS Input = JPEG

Input = Postgis Input = OGR Input = GDAL Input = Shapefile

Installation Instructions

1. To install the MS4W zip file, use a compression programme (*e.g.*, WinZip) to extract the package at the root of a drive, *e.g.*, drives C:\. If successful, a new directory named 'ms4w' will be created at the root of the drive you chose (*e.g.*, C:/ms4w).
2. Start MS4W Apache Web Server by running /ms4w/apache-install.bat (at the command line or by double-clicking it). This file installs Apache as a Windows service (called 'Apache Web Server') so that it starts whenever the computer is restarted. When executed, a DOS window should pop up with the following message:

::

Installing the Apache MS4W Web Server service

The Apache MS4W Web Server service is successfully installed.

Testing httpd.conf....

Errors reported here must be corrected before the service can be started.

The Apache MS4W Web Server service is starting.

The Apache MS4W Web Server service was started successfully.

This means that Apache is running and installed as a service.

(a) Special Notes for Win95, 98, and ME

Users of Win95, 98, and ME will not be able to install Apache as a service. Instead Apache should be manually started each time, by clicking on /ms4w/Apache/bin/httpd.exe. An empty DOS window will open, which means Apache is running. To stop Apache close the empty DOS window.

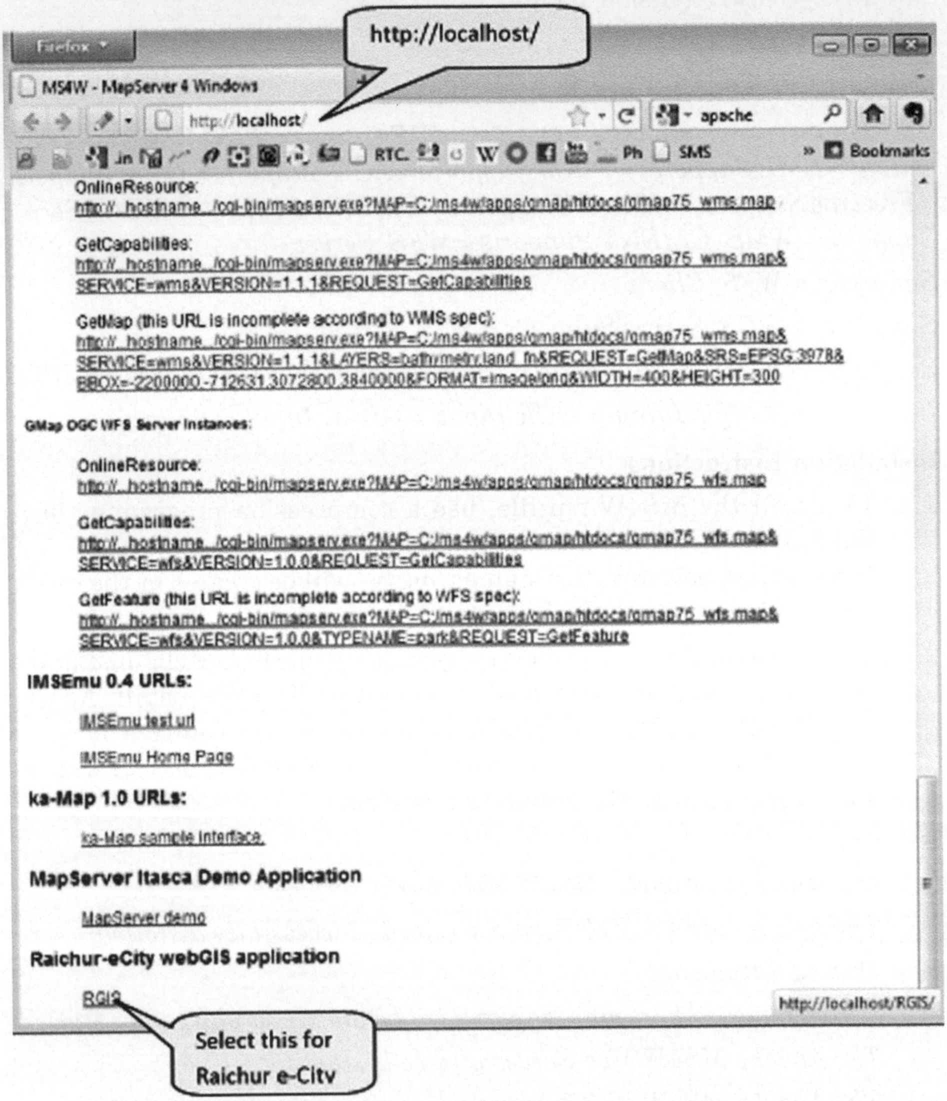

Fig. 8.3: Firefox web Browser Displaying the web page of MS4W (Mapserver). Note the link of Raichur e-City Application

(b) *Special Notes for Microsoft Vista*

In order to run the apache-install.bat file, you must do the following:

- In Windows Explorer, got the location of your cmd.exe file (C:/ Windows/System32).
- Right-click the cmd.exe executable and choose 'Run as Administrator'.
- Navigate to ms4w folder in the command prompt window and run apache-install.bat.

3. To test that Apache is running properly, open your Web browser and find your local host Web service by entering one of the following URLs:

   http://localhost/

   or

   http://127.0.0.1/

The main MS4W page would open up in the Web browser. This gives general information about the installation along with configuration information. Review the listed 'Features' installed within MS4W, and test them by selecting each link found on this page (Figure 8.3).

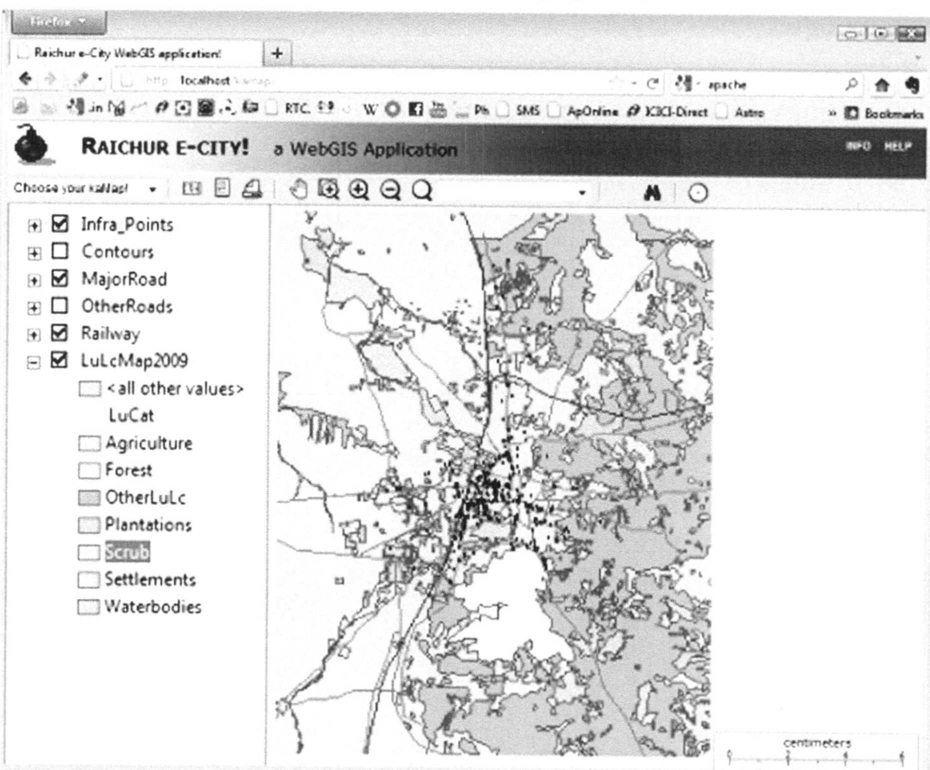

Fig. 8.4: Firefox web Browser Displaying the Webclient - *Raichur e-City,* Web GIS Application, Powered by Ka-Map 1.0

4. Technically, at this point *MS4W* and *Raichur e-City* is installed. Select the link: *Raichur e-City* to use the web-GIS application of Raichur city (Figure 8.4).

TESTING AND IMPLEMENTATION

'Raichur e-City' software package was subjected to the following tests and the requisite changes were done till repeated use of the software by all-comers brought forth no hitch or discomfort. This involved testing of each individual programme segment for general robustness of the system.

The software package was subjected to unit testing, function testing, performance testing and integration.

- *Unit Testing:* All the individual aspects of the programme were tested to check the performance of the intended function.
- *Functional Testing*: Functional test involved testing the system under typical operating conditions, typical input values and for typical expected results. The functional boundary specifies the framework within which the system can function.

SUMMARY

'Raichur e-City' has been developed which significantly contributes to the existing GIS database by using the concept of free and open source GIS software. This application demonstrates the advancements achieved in the area of web-GIS.

9

CONCLUSIONS AND RECOMMENDATIONS

CONCLUSIONS

Raichur city is a rapidly growing city with strong economic base in agriculture, commerce and industry. Raichur is the largest urban centre and district headquarter of Raichur District with considerable tourism potential due to its antiquity.

The city is best owed with extremities in terms of climate and geographical settings. Raichur, located in the proximity of two major rivers has the potential for agrarian land-use, while the uncertain rainfall pattern makes agriculture vulnerable to the vagaries of nature.

Though the city is young, already there are indicators pointing towards the rampant and uncontrolled growth in terms of built-up area and geo-demographics. In view of this, the present study assumes significance in understanding the impact of urban sprawl on various aspects of Raichur city in terms of demography, socio-economics, land-use and land-cover using GIS, remote sensing and urban sprawl metrics and dynamics. The major conclusions of the study are as follows:

1. *Land-use and Land-cover;* Agriculture is the predominant land-use pattern followed by stony waste, water resources and settlements. The present agrarian land-use of Raichur city is under imminent threat

from the rapid and burgeoning urbanization. Considering the present trend, by 2021, nearly 27 per cent of the agricultural land would be converted to settlements. The steady increase of the built-up area in spite of the decreasing decadal growth rate points to the horizontal expansion of the city, where the land is consumed at an excessive rate by the same population.

2. *Demography and Socio-economic Indicators:* As per the estimates of induced growth rate, the Raichur population for 2021 has been calculated as total of 5,00,000 people. The burgeoning population, wide gender disparity in adult and child literacy, and large non-worker population are matters of serious concern and have to be addressed on priority basis.
3. *Infrastructure:* Infrastructure of Raichur city has been examined under the various categories of social, socio-cultural, economic, and physical. The salient findings of the assessment are:
    - *literacy:* the poor child and female literacy rates are a major concern that needs to be addressed on priority basis;
    - *health:* considering the projected population of 2,65,000 for 2011, the existing medical infrastructure is not adequate. Also, the existing medical infrastructure such as: nursing homes are not distributed geographically, rather they are concentrated in the core of the city;
    - *parks and playgrounds:* the city lacks adequate parks and playgrounds. Also, the schools and colleges do not have adequate play grounds;
    - *agriculture:* the city has good agriculture infrastructure in place with well identified market areas, sub markets, rural markets coordinated through the market committee;
    - *industry:* considering the abundance of natural resources such as: minerals, water resources, power, land availability, human resources; and very good connectivity by road and rail, Raichur has great potential to emerge as strong industrial base. The proximity of Hyderabad is an added advantage;

The Yeramarus Thermal Power Station (YTPS), Surana Industries (P) Ltd., Vishweshwaryya Steel plant and Central Power Grid Station are coming up shortly which would provide much required thrust for economic growth.

- *solid waste management*: The integrated solid waste management project for Raichur city, sponsored by Indo-Norwegian Environment Programme and Directorate of Municipal administration, has come as breather for the citizens. Under this programme, CMC Raichur in partnership with ASTRA (IISc, Bangalore) and Environment Support Group have taken the solid waste management of the city;

- *traffic and transportation:* two wheelers constitute majority of the city traffic due to the lack of proper mass transit system;

The road pattern, insufficient road width, and bad intersections at important places are causing traffic snarls and hazards. The crowded areas such as: Mahaveer chowk, vegetable market, Teen Khandeel circle have very narrow roads with poor road surface. The city lacks dedicated parking lots.

4. *Metrics and Dynamics of Urban Sprawl.* Based on the spatial pattern, the sprawl of Raichur can be categorised as that of compact development type with ribbon type of development along the SH 13 (Hyderabad Road) and SH 20 (Lingasugur Road).

Shannon's entropy correlates well with the progressive built-up area across the years. The computation of patchiness revealed that about 57.14 per cent of the study area is homogeneous.

High and low density built-up areas were found all along the highways along with the city centres. Most of the high density areas were found to be within and closer to the core of Raichur city. However, medium density areas were found mostly along the city periphery. This further substantiates the results of Shannon's entropy, which revealed high dispersion of the built-up theme in the study area.

5. *3D Mapping:* The surface elevation model of the city using TIN indicates that nearly 58 per cent of the city is relatively flat with elevations ranging from 355 to 391 m. Digital terrain Model of Raichur city has been developed with the ward boundaries overlaid as soft fill. An overview of DTM of Raichur reveals that highest altitudes were found at the South East corner of the city and the terrain undulates from the highest elevation of 520 m on the south East to 355 m towards north and northwest.

Slope analysis indicates that most of the landscape is predominantly flat. The steepest slope was identified in the hilly terrains located in the southeast part of the city.

6. *Developing Web GIS Application:* Raichur e-City has complete database about the city such as: cadastral information, demographic information, Raichur road network, and land-use information in detail. The software application can help to a large extent to design number of applications, planning procedures, and to manage urban areas efficiently.

As a long-term goal, Raichur e-City will help to address various issues related to development of civic amenities and infrastructure in Raichur.

The same can be utilized for enforcement of law and can play a vital role in decision support system.

RECOMMENDATIONS

By consolidating the findings from the present research and keeping in view, the major problems of the city, certain measures have been suggested for the efficient monitoring and implementation of the development plans for Raichur city.

Raichur city needs a vision. A vision that can project how the city would look like in the coming 20 years and what really matters for the people living in the city. The existing document – *The vision 2020 of Raichur city*, merely looks at the demographic aspects of the city and what infrastructure would be required to meet their demands. For achieving the goal of a better city, it requires a deeper understanding of the priorities of the people living in-and-around Raichur, the government and the nation as a whole.

Appropriate land use policies need to be created for the efficient and sustainable growth of the city. Zoning of the land is one such device of land use planning used by local governments in most of the countries. Zoning a city into residential, commercial, and industrial would be useful in preventing development from interfering with existing residents or business and to preserve the character of a community.

Some of the very critical aspects which need immediate attention are:

- As per the guidelines of *Urban Development Plans Formulation and Implementation Guidelines* (UDPFI), in the next couple of years Raichur would require another 10 pre-primary schools, one integrated school without hostel facility and one with hostel facility, and a special school for handicapped.
- The city needs another three intermediate hospitals. It is recommended that any new medical facilities that are likely to come up, and even possibly relocate the existing ones, such that all the residents of the city can have access to them with least effort.
- To fulfil the basic infrastructure criteria of UDPFI, the city needs another 12 community halls, 53 community rooms, one more recreation club, and one more socio-cultural centre.
- The crowded areas such as: Mahaveer chowk, vegetable market, Teen Khandeel circle have very narrow roads with poor road surface. These roads need to be widened and resurfaced for easy and quick traffic flow. As the pedestrian traffic is also more in these areas, special provision must be made for pedestrians. Traffic circles at important road junctions need to be redesigned. Road side trees help increase the

aesthetic look of the roads and also they bring down the pollution levels and local temperatures. Thus, road side plantations need to be taken up on the existing and upcoming roads.

- Bus stand, Gunj Road, Market area, and teen Khandeel Circle need immediate provision for parking. The authorities need to ensure that the existing shopping malls, restaurants and cinema halls to have adequate parking space. And it should be ensured that all the new buildings be sanctioned for construction only after assurance of adequate parking facilities.
- The GIS data need to be updated on regular basis to check the deviations in the land-use with respect to what has been proposed in the development plans.
- Identify illegal encroachments along the hill slopes and the water bodies in order to stop the unregulated and unplanned development.
- It is prime time to check for any violation in the development plans and to regularise the construction activities with the help of spatial technologies. Laying down stipulations for the private real estate developers to ensure construction of wide roads within the layout and also proper approach roads to the housing societies. This would subsequently help the corporation authorities to extend services and amenities like: public transport, drainage facility, garbage collection and disposal etc.
- Rainwater harvesting has to be made mandatory in all the new construction areas, so that depleting ground water level can be arrested.
- The green spaces of the city have to be restored and developed. This can be done by taking up afforestation on the barren hill slopes. Green belts absorb large quantities of atmospheric pollution especially 'particulates', which will help to reduce the pollution level. In the fringe villages, setting up of biotechnology parks and agro-zones would restrict the illegal development in these areas.
- Solid waste can be recycled and even used for power generation. GIS can help to find suitable sites for such purposes.

There are many non-governmental organizations (NGO) working independently for the betterment of city. These programmes have to be co-ordinated and channelized for building a better city and society.

More thrust on the use of GIS for day-to-day utility applications like: power sector, drainage and sewerage network can increase the efficiency of administrative machinery many folds. Educational institutes and Government organizations can help in this and by providing proper training to the bureaucrats and decision-making authorities in chalking out management strategies. However, for finding solutions to any problem, the appropriate measures have to be taken not only by the planning authorities but also by the public who live in the city. A positive attitude of the residents and their co-operation with the planning authorities in maintaining the environs of the city and making it more livable would definitely make a huge difference to the city.

REFERENCES

1. PRB (Population Reference Bureau), World Population Highlights, 2007: Urbanization.

   Website: *http://www.prb.org/Articles/2007/623Urbanization.aspx*
2. Nelson A.C. and Duncan J.B., Growth Management Principles and Practices, Planners Press, Chicago, IL, 1995.
3. Ottensmann J.R., Urban Sprawl, Land Values and the Density of Development, *Land Economics*, 53 (4): 1977, pp. 389-400.
4. Ewing R., Is Los Angeles-Style Sprawl Desirable? *Journal of the American Planning Association*, 63: 1997, pp. 107-126.
5. Galster G., Hansan R., Ratcliffe M., Wolman H., Coleman S., and Freihage J., Wrestling Sprawl to the Ground: Defining and Measuring an Elusive Concept, Housing Policy Debate, 12: 2001, pp. 681-718.
6. Alanso W., Location and Land Use: Toward a General Theory of Land Rent, Harvard University Press, Cambridge, MA, 1964.
7. Mills E.S., The Value of Urban Land, pp. 231-253, in Perlott H. S. (Ed.), The Quality of the Urban Environment, Johns Hopkins, Baltimore, 1971.
8. Knaap G.J., The Price Effects of an Urban Growth Boundary in Metropolitan Portland, Oregon, *Land Economics*, 61: 1985, pp. 26-35.
9. Von Thunen J.H., Isolated State: An English Edition of der Isolierte Staat, Ed. P. Hall, Pergamon Press, Oxford, 1966.

10. Peiser R.B., Does It Pay To Plan Suburban Development? *Journal of the American Planning Association*, 50: 1984, pp. 419-433.
11. Fischel W.A., Introduction: Four Maxims For Research on Landuse Controls, Land Economics, 66: 1990, pp. 229-236.
12. Moss W.G., Large Lot Zoning, Property Taxes and Metropolitan Area, *Journal of Urban Economics*, 4: 1977, pp. 408-427.
13. Sheppard E.S., The Search For Flexible Theory: Comments On Cadwallader, Urban Geography, 9:1988, pp. 225-264.
14. Pendall R., Do Land-Use Controls Cause Sprawl? Environment and Planning B: Planning and Design, 26: 1999, pp. 555-71.
15. Peterson U. and Raivo A., Changes in Agricultural Land use in Estonia in the 1990's, Detected with Multitemporal Landsat MSS Imagery, Landscape and Urban Planning, 41: 1998, pp. 193-201.
16. Allen J. and Lu K., Modeling and Prediction of Future Urban Growth in the Charleston Region of South Carolina: A GIS-based Integrated Approach, Conservation Ecology, 8 (2): 2003, pp. 2.
17. Farooq S. and Ahmad S., Urban Sprawl Development around Aligarh City: A Study Aided by Satellite Remote Sensing and GIS, *J. Indian Soc. Remote Sens.*, 36: 2008, pp. 77-88.
18. Nechyba T.J. and Walsh R.P., Urban Sprawl, *Journal of Economic Perspectives*, 18 (4): 2004, pp. 177-200.
19. Hathout S., The Use of GIS for Monitoring and Predicting Urban Growth in East and West St. Paul, Winnipeg, Manitoba, Canada, *Journal of Environmental Management*, 66: 2002, pp. 229-238.
20. Wilson E.H., Hurd J.D., Civco D.L., Prisloe M. P. and Arnold C., Development of a Geospatial Model to Quantify, Describe and Map Urban Growth, Remote Sensing of Environment, 86: 2003, pp. 275-285.
21. Howard F., Urban Sprawl and Public Health, Public Health Reports, 117: 2002, pp. 201-217.
22. Rathbone V.B. and Huckabee J.C., Controlling Road Rage: A Literature Review and Pilot Study, AAA Foundation for Traffic Safety, Washington, 1999.
23. Howard F., Lawrence F., Richard J. and Russ L., Urban Sprawl and Public Health: Designing, Planning, Building for Healthy Communities, Island Press, 2004, 338 pages.
24. Putnam R.D., Bowling Alone: The Collapse and Revival of American Community, Simon and Schuster, New York, 2000.

25. Burchell R.W., Lowenstein G., Dolphin W.R., Galley C.C., Downs A., Seskin S., Still K.G. and Moore T., Costs of Sprawl - 2000, TCRP Report 74, Transportation Research Board, National Research Council, National Academy Press, 2002, p. 100.

26. Ahmad N. M. L. and Yaakup A., Scenario-based Spatial Modelling for Land use Planning and Valuation.

Website: *http://www.gisdevelopment.net/application/urban/sprawl/mm060.htm*

27. Ewing R., Characteristics, Causes and Effects of Sprawl: A Literature Review, Environmental and Urban Issues, FAU/FIU Joint Centre, 1994.

28. Johnson M.P., Environmental Impacts of Urban Sprawl: A Survey of the Literature and Proposed Research Agenda, *Environment and Planning*, 33(4): 2001, pp. 717-736.

29. Nelson A.C., Comparing States with and without Growth Management: Analysis Based on Indicators with Policy Implications, Land Use Policy, 16: 1999, pp. 121-127.

30. Kline J., Comparing States with and without Growth Management: Analysis Based on Indicators with Policy Implication Comment, Land Use Policy: 17, 2000, pp. 349-355.

31. Hurd J.D, Wilson E.H., Lammey S. G. and Civeo D.L., Characterization of Forest Fragmentation and Urban Sprawl Using Time Sequential Landsat Imagery, Proc. ASPRS Annual Convention, St. Louis, MO, April 23-27, 2001.

32. NAUTILUS, Characterization of Urban Sprawl, 2001.

Website: *http:/iresac.uconn.edu/research/urban Sprawl/index.htm*

33. Yeh A.G.O. and Xia Li, Measurement and Monitoring of Urban Sprawl in a Rapidly Growing Region Using Entropy, Photogrammetric Engineering and Remote Sensing, 67(1): 2001, pp. 83.

34. Almeida Berkley, A GIS Assessment of Urban Sprawl in Richmond, Virginia, MS Thesis, Virginia Polytechnic Institute and State University, Blacksburg, 2005, pp. 141.

35. Sierra Club, Debate on Theories of David Rusk, The Regionalist, 2(3) 1997.

Website: *http://www.sierraclub.org/sprawl/population.asp*

36. Berry B. J. L., Urbanisation, pp. 103-119, in Turner II B. L., Clark W.C., Kates R.W., Richards J.F., Mathews J.T. and Meyer W.B. (Eds.), The Earth as Transformed by Human Action, Cambridge University Press, U.K., 1990.

37. Barnes K. B., Morgan II J. M., Roberge M. C. and Lowe S., Sprawl Development: It's Patterns, Consequences, and Measurement, Towson University.

Website: *http://chesapeake, towson edu/landscape/urbansprawl/download/Sprawl_white_paper.pdf 2001.*

38. Epstein J., Payne K. and Kramer E., Techniques for Mapping Suburban Sprawl, Photogrammetric Engineering and Remote Sensing, 63(9): 2002, pp. 913-918.

39. Sutton P., Roberts D., Elvidge C. and Meij H., A Comparison of Night-Time Satellite Imagery and Population Density for the Continental United States, Photogrammetric Engineering and Remote Sensing, 63(11): 1997, pp. 1303-1313.

40. Welch R., Monitoring Urban Population and Energy Utilization Patterns from Satellite Data, Remote Sensing of Environment, 9: 1980, pp. 1-9.

41. Saravanan P. and Ilangovan P., Identification of Urban Sprawl Pattern for Madurai Region Using GIS, *International Journal of Geomatics and Geosciences*, 1(2): 2010, pp. 141-149.

42. Forman R.T.T., Land Mosaic: The Ecology of Landscapes and Regions, Cambridge University Press, New York, 1995.

43. Mc Garigal K., Cushman S. A., Neel M. C. and Ene E., FRAGSTATS: Spatial Pattern Analysis Programme for Categorical Maps, Computer Software Programme Produced by the Authors at the University of Massachusetts, Amherst, 2002.

Website: *http://www.umass.edu/landeco/research/fragstats/fragstats.html*

44. Thomas R.W., Information Statistics in Geography, Geo Abstracts, University of East Anglia, Norwich, United Kingdom, 1981, pp. 42.

45. Lata K.M., Krishna P.V., Badrinath K.V.S., Raghavaswamy V. and Sankar Rao C.H., Measuring Urban Sprawl: A Case Study of Hyderabad, GIS Development, 5(12): 2001, pp. 26-29.

46. Sudhira H.S., Ramachandra T.V. and Jagadish K.S, Urban Sprawl: Metrics, Dynamics and Modeling using GIS, *International Journal of Applied Earth Observation and Geoinformation*, 5:2004, pp. 29-39.

47. Batty M., Xie Y. and Sun Z., Modeling Urban Dynamics Through GIS-Based Cellular Automata, Computers, *Environment and Urban Systems*, 23: 1999, pp. 205-233.

48. Torrens P.M. and Alberti M., Measuring Sprawl, Working Paper No. 27, Centre for Advanced Spatial Analysis, University College London, 2000.

Website: *http://www.casa.ac.uk/working papers/*

49. Website: *http://maps.google.co.in/*
50. Website: *http://www.raichur.in/*
51. Meteorological Observatory, Raichur, Karnataka.
52. Raichur Urban Development Authority, Master Plan-2021, Revision-I, for Raichur Local Planning Area, 2008, pp. 144.
53. Director of Census Operations, District Census Handbook 2001, Government Press Karnataka.
54. Website: *http://www.meraraichur.com/*
55. Website: *http://en.wikipedia.org/wiki/Raichur_district*
56. Census of India, *http://www.censusindia.net*
57. CGWB, Ground Water Information Booklet, Raichur District, Karnataka, Central Ground Water Board, South Western Region, 2008.
58. Eryilmaz S.S., Cengiz H. and Eryilmaz Y., The Urban Sprawl Model for An Affected Metroplolis: Bursa – Istanbul Example, 44th ISoCaRP Congress: 2008.
59. Gadal S., Fournier S. and Emeric P., 3D Dynamic Representation for Urban Sprawl Modeling: Example of India's Delhi-Mumbai Corridor, S.A.P.I.E.N.S, 2009.

    Website: *http://sapiens.revues.org/index932.html*
60. Hasse J., Using Remote Sensing and GIS Integration to Identify Spatial Characteristics of Sprawl at the Building-unit Level, pp. 117-143, in Mesev V (Ed.)., Integration of GIS and Remote Sensing, John Wiley and Sons, New York, V: 2007.
61. Jenness J., Tools for Graphics and Shapes: Extension for ArcGIS, Jenness Enterprises, 2010.

    Website: *http://www.jennessent.com/arcgis/shapes_graphics.htm*
62. Kumar J.M., Garg P.K. and Khare D., Monitoring and Modeling of Urban Sprawl Using Remote Sensing and GIS Techniques, *International Journal of Applied Earth Observation and Geoinformation*, 10 (1): 2008, pp. 26-43.
63. Pilouk M.A. and Abdul R (Eds.), Spatial Data Modelling for 3D GIS, Springer Berlin Heidelberg, Berlin, 2007.
64. Rashed T., An Integrative GIS and Remote Sensing Model for Place-based Urban Vulnerability Analysis, pp. 199-224, in Mesev V. (Ed.), Integration of GIS and Remote Sensing, John Wiley and Sons, New York, V:2007.

65. Website: *http://en.wikipedia.org/wiki/Apache_HTTP_Server*
66. USEPA, Urban Sprawl Modeling, Air Quality Monitoring and Risk Communication, The Northeast Ohio Project, United States Environmental Protection Agency, 2002.
67. Yang X., Integrating Remote Sensing, GIS and Spatial Modelling for Sustainable Urban Growth Management, pp. 173-193, in Mesev V. (Ed.), Integration of GIS and Remote Sensing, John Wiley and Sons, New York, V: 2007.
68. Hu Q. and Hu M.Y., Semantics-based 3D Dynamic Hierarchical House Property Model, *International Journal of Geographical Information Science*, 24(2): 2008, pp. 165-188.
69. Dharmalingam A. and Morgan P. S, Women's Work, Autonomy and Birth Control: Evidence from Two South Indian Villages, Population Studies, 50: 1996, pp. 187-201.
70. Sullivan A. and Steven M. S., Economics: Principles in Action, Pearson Prentice Hall, 2003, pp. 474.
71. American Heritage Dictionary of the English Language, Houghton Mifflin Company, 2006.
72. UDPFI, Urban Development Plans Formulation and Implementation Guidelines, Ministry of Urban Affairs and Employment, Government of India, New Delhi, 1996. Website: *http://education.yahoo.com/reference/dictionary/entry/infrastructure*
73. Census of India, Population Projections for India and States 2001-26, 2006, pp. 268.

    Website: *http://nrhm-is.nic.in/UI/Public%20Periodic/Population_Projection_Report_2006.pdf*
74. Breuekner J.K., Urban Sprawl: Diagnosis and Remedies, *International Regional Science Review*, 23(2): 2000, pp. 160-171.
75. Li Xia and Yeh Gar-On, Analyzing Spatial Restructuring of Land use Patterns in a Fast Growing Region using Remote Sensing and GIS, Landscape and Urban Planning 69: 2004, pp. 335-354.
76. Website: *https://secure1.securityspace.com/s_survey/data/man.200907/apacheos.html*
77. Batty M., Xie Y. and Sun Z., The Dynamics of Urban Sprawl, Working Paper Series, Paper 15, Centre for Advanced Spatial Analysis, University College, London, 1999. Website: http://www.casa.ac.uk/working papers/.
78. Torrens P.M. and Sullivan D O., Cellular Automata and Urban Simulation: Where do we go from here? Environmental Planning B: Planning and Design, 28:2001, pp. 163-168.

79. McGarigal K. and B.J. Marks., FRAGSTATS: Spatial Pattern Analysis Programme for Quantifying Landscape Structure, Gen. Tech. Rep. PNW-GTR-351, Portland, OR: U.S. Department of Agriculture, Forest Service, Pacific Northwest Research Station, 1995, pp. 122.
80. Gustafson E.J., Quantifying Landscape Spatial Pattern: What is the State of the art? *Ecosystems* 1: 1998, pp. 143-156.
81. Murphy D.L., Estimating Neighborhood Variability with a Binary Comparison Matrix, Photogrammetry, *Eng. Remote Sens.*, 51(6): 1985, pp. 667-674.
82. Website: *http://en.wikipedia.org/wiki/Maps*
83. James Swanson, The Three Dimensional Visualization and Analysis of Geographic Data. Website: *http://maps.unomaha.edu/Peterson/gis/Final_Projects/1996/Swanson/GIS_Paper.html*
84. Website: *http://www.esri.com/library/brochures/pdfs/gis-for-green-government.pdf*
85. Jain M., GIS and Remote Sensing for Urban Sprawl and Planning, 2009.

    Website:http://www.vector1media.com/article/features/7538-gis-and-remote-sensing-for-urban-sprawl-and-planning.html
86. Xianfeng S., Yasuyuki K. and Mamoru S., The Development of web Mapping Application Using Open Source GIS Solution, International Symposium on Geoinformatics for Spatial Infrastructure Development in Earth and Allied Sciences, 2004.
87. Jeff McKenna, An Introduction to MapServer, 2006.

    Website: *http://mapserver.org/introduction.html#contents*
88. Quantum GIS User Guide, 1.7.0 'Wroclaw'.

    Website: *http://download.osgeo.org/qgis/doc/manual/qgis-1.7.0_user_guide_en.pdf*
89. Website: *http://spatialserver.net/qgis2ms/#toc2*
90. Website: *http://ka-map-omniverdi.org/wiki/index.php/mainpage.*

INDEX

□□□□